Creating a
NEW OLD HOUSE

Creating a
NEW OLD HOUSE

YESTERDAY'S CHARACTER FOR TODAY'S HOME

RUSSELL VERSACI, AIA

Photographs by Erik Kvalsvik

The Taunton Press

To my parents, Armand and Nancy Versaci,
who instructed me as a young boy that
"cream always rises" so "just make a game of it."
I finally understand!

THE AMERICAN INSTITUTE
OF ARCHITECTS

The American Institute of Architects, founded in 1857, is a professional society of architects with over 70,000 members in the United States and abroad. Through its national, regional, state, and local components, the AIA works to achieve more humane built environments and higher standards of professionalism for architects through education, government advocacy, community redevelopment, and public outreach activities. AIA's website is located at aia.org.

AIA, The American Institute of Architects, and the AIA logo are registered trademarks and service marks of The American Institute of Architects.

This book is published under the joint imprint of The American Institute of Architects and The Taunton Press, Inc.

Text © 2003 by Russell Versaci
Photographs © 2003 by Erik Kvalsvik except where noted: Hallmark photo p. 28 courtesy of George Washington Smith, Architecture & Design Collection, University Art Museum, University of California, Santa Barbara; Hallmark photo p. 39 courtesy of Library of Congress, Prints & Photographs Division, HABS, AK, 23-MCKIN, 3-2; Hallmark photo p. 50 courtesy of Library of Congress, Prints & Photographs Division,, HABS, NM, 31-ACOMP, 1-52; Hallmark photo p. 63 courtesy of Library of Congress, Prints & Photographs Division, HABS, ILL, 4-, 1-1; Hallmark photo p. 73 courtesy of the Preston Historical Society, Preston, CT; Hallmark photo p. 85 courtesy of Library of Congress, Prints & Photographs Division, HABS, PA, 6-BAUM.V, 1-4; Hallmark photo p. 97 courtesy of Library of Congress, Prints & Photographs Division, HABS, MASS, B-WILBU, 1-2; Hallmark photo p. 121 courtesy of Library of Congress, Prints & Photographs Division, HABS, MD, 22-HAGTO, 2-14; Hallmark photo p. 133 courtesy of Library of Congress, Prints & Photographs Division, HABS, MASS, 1-ORLS, 1-1; Hallmark photo p. 163 © Jerry Ripberger, Louisiana Images; Hallmark photo p. 188 courtesy of Library of Congress, Prints & Photographs Division, HABS, LA, 39-NEWRO.V, 1-2; Hallmark photo p. 199 © Alexander Vertikoff; Hallmark photo p. 205 © Richard McNamee, Studiorichard.com; Hallmark photo p. 209 courtesy of Library of Congress, Prints & Photographs Division, HABS, ME, 3-PORT, 17-11. Illustrations © 2003 by The Taunton Press, Inc.

The Taunton Press
Inspiration for hands-on living®

The Taunton Press, Inc.63 South Main Street, PO Box 5506, Newtown, CT 06470-5506
e-mail: tp@taunton.com

Distributed by Publishers Group West

EDITOR: Marilyn Zelinsky Syarto
JACKET/COVER DESIGN: Dania Davey
INTERIOR DESIGN: Dania Davey
LAYOUT: Dania Davey, Carol Petro
ILLUSTRATOR: André Paul Junget
PHOTOGRAPHER: Erik Kvalsvik, except where otherwise noted

Library of Congress Cataloging-in-Publication Data

Versaci, Russell.
  Creating a new old house : yesterday's character for today's home /
Russell Versaci ; photographs by Erik Kvalsvik.
    p. cm.
  ISBN 1-56158-615-3
 1. Architecture, Domestic--Conservation and restoration--United
States. I. Title.
  NA7205.V47 2003
  728'.37'0288--dc21
                                    200300499

Printed in Singapore
10 9 8 7 6 5 4 3 2 1

A book, like a work of architecture, is the creative product of many hands in which the author is but one small part. I am an accidental writer, having for two decades enjoyed a career in designing houses without writing more than a few words about my work. I required substantial encouragement from my muse, Kathie Friedley, before deciding I could ever document in words the concepts I had formerly expressed only in wood and stone.

I am indebted to my partners in architecture, David Neumann and Mark Buchanan, for supporting me with time to write this book. They have made it possible for me to take a two-year sabbatical from our practice to share our common philosophy of design.

During my search for the finest houses to portray in this portfolio, many friends have shared their collective knowledge of architects, notably Philip Morris of *Southern Accents*, Clem Labine of *Period Homes*, and Daniel Gregory of *Sunset*. My valued colleagues in traditional architecture have offered their professional insights as well, including Gilbert Schafer of the Institute for Classical Architecture and John Massengale of the Institute of Traditional Architecture. And more than 125 architects have kindly furnished examples of their work for my consideration and directed me to their compatriots in search of new old houses.

The artistic essence of good architecture is difficult to convey in photographs. I have been fortunate to have architectural photographer Erik Kvalsvik join me to document these houses. Erik has an artist's eye and an instinctive appreciation for capturing images that tell the story, as well as an affable wit that often soothed frayed nerves on hours of cross-country flights.

I am grateful to The Taunton Press for taking a chance on my unproven skills as a writer and showing me where to begin. Throughout the writing of the manuscript, the editorial team has provided me with invaluable direction. Book development editor, Marilyn Zelinsky Syarto, has been both a cheerleader urging me forward and a stern task master challenging me to dig deeper for substance. What consistency of thought and meaningful insights are in the text are the result of her patient encouragement. Art director, Paula Schlosser, has translated my vision for the book as a timeless classic into the exquisite pages enclosed between these covers.

I am most grateful to all the homeowners who allowed me to photograph their private homes and to tell the story of crafting their new old houses. Their shared experiences will inspire many others, who I hope will profit by their example.

Finally, throughout two years of traveling and writing, I am grateful to my son, Dudley, who endured my part-time fathering with understanding and even a bit of pride in my authorship

BUILDING NEW TRADITIONS

"Let's find a great old house and fix it up." Perhaps you daydream of living in a home with a past. But in real life, you know that the adventure of rebuilding an old house often leads down a rocky road. By creating a new old house, you can skirt these troubles and satisfy your old-house soul. This book will show you the path to a new home that is patterned on tradition.

Two decades ago in architecture school I discovered my own passion for things old. At the time, Modernism was the rule of the day. The spare forms of Modern American homes did not have the connection to the old-fashioned arts and crafts that made traditional houses delightful places to live. In the world of Modernism, I was a lost soul.

Disenchanted, I turned to history for inspiration. While searching through dusty volumes in the library, I uncovered treasures. America was rich with forgotten styles, from the first colonial dwellings and styles of the new republic through early-twentieth-century classicism. Determined to rediscover the legacy of the past, I decided to make a career out of designing homes built on tradition.

LONGING FOR AN OLD HOUSE Like many of you, my clients long to recreate the gracious homes of the past. In pursuit of their dreams, we have brought to life the new old house, a vintage home designed for modern living. We have unearthed forgotten details of style, building techniques, and materials with timeless character and integrated them with the benefits of modern conveniences. The houses we have created are new variations on classic styles, blending the emotional comforts of the past with the creature comforts of today.

TIMELESS PILLARS As an architect, I delight in the complexity of designing houses. In the process, I have learned ways of building "new old," which have become my working tools. I call these principles the Pillars of Traditional Design. The Pillars are design principles drawn from the old ways of building which seamlessly weave the past into the present.

The houses in these pages have been created by architects, builders, and homeowners who are dedicated to making new old houses. These homes represent rich geographic diversity of regional styles in America. You will see portraits of seventeen new houses in the traditional styles of our forefathers: from the native forms of the Southwest and Spanish settlements in Florida and California, to the early architecture of the colonies from New England to Georgia, through the Greek Revival style, to the pioneer traditions of Texas and the Rocky Mountains.

These outstanding examples, selected from more than 300 homes, present the way traditional American styles are being reinterpreted in the best new homes of today. My hope is that they will inspire you to create the new old house of your dreams, wherever you may live.

REVIVING
THE CLASSIC HOMES OF
THE PAST

There is mystery in the character of an old house—in the painted clapboard, mottled brick, and weathered slate as well as in the faded wallpaper, mellowed floorboards, and hand-rubbed hardware. An old house has a soul nurtured by the passage of time.

The front porch is a classic hallmark of the romance of an old house, an open invitation to hospitality and gracious living. The porch of this new Southern plantation is carved under a deep roof and surrounded by rich architectural details.

Timeless patterns in the way old houses are put together can become a template for making something new from something old.

Our childhood memories are colored with picture-postcard images of old houses. Most of us can remember dreamlike visions of the house we grew up in or wish we had. We recall the pleasures of sultry days at a summerhouse spent idling on the front porch or swinging from the big tree in the backyard. Or Sunday drives in the country peering out the car window in wonder at the picket fences of time-worn old farmhouses as we flew by. These scenes from the past, which are half-remembered and half-imagined, come to the surface when we dream about building a new home.

Creating a new house ought to be like walking down memory lane, gathering these treasured recollections for one of life's most creative endeavors. Yet imagining a new house can be daunting. Many people are confounded by the idea of building— wondering what the house should look like, how to make it feel comfortable, and whether it will reflect a personal style.

We tour new homes looking for ideas, yet most of the new houses are cookie-cutter copies and ordinary. Combing through the bookstore shelves for inspiration, we find glossy photos of houses that seem too fussy and grand or too spare and monastic. In our search for the perfect image, we realize that a weave of textures with the patina of age acquires a seductive charm that draws us irresistibly toward old houses.

OLD HOUSE REALITY CHECK

Many of us have discovered a delightfully neglected old farmhouse on a drive in the country, and feel our heart skip a beat. "If only I could live there! That's my house," we fantasize. And we start to think that the house of our dreams is really an old house. Yet real old houses come with real drawbacks.

Too often the fixer-upper is just a pretty shell of a house. Many old houses are too far gone to be salvaged without major rebuilding. There are gaping holes in the floorboards, the fireplace bricks are scattered across the parlor floor, and there is daylight

Although this house looks old, it is really a new house meant to resemble an eighteenth-century original meticulously restored for modern living. The German stone farmhouse is located on a piece of property that is filled with old oak trees, an element of nature that adds a patina of age to this home.

Creating a new old house with a traditional pedigree is possible when you follow a set of imaginative guidelines to re-create the classic features of an old house. A new Gulf Coast cottage built with authentic details and recycled antique materials looks so convincing that one elderly neighbor swears it has been there since her childhood.

where the back wall used to be. Structural timbers are rotted, the roof leaks, and the wiring is outdated—myriad basic repairs need to be done simply to make the house livable. There are just too many problems to solve, and most homeowners have neither the will nor the wallet to tackle them.

A NEW HOUSE WITH A PAST

What we really want is a brand new house wrapped in the raiment of an old house. The house must be seasoned by the past, but its inner workings must be up to the minute. Not willing to do without modern conveniences and creature comforts, we want indoor plumbing, plenty of closets, and an efficient heating system. And we want the new amenities of a gourmet kitchen, family room, and home office. Yet we want all of this newness covered in layers of vintage tradition that breathe the comforting air of history. The answer is a *new old house.*

A new old house combines the emotional comforts of yesterday with the creature comforts of today. A new home can be crafted with the familiar forms and harmonious proportions of tradition and also be planned for convenience and tailored for modern

family living. There are timeless patterns in the way old houses are put together, which can become a template for making something new from something old.

After years of designing new houses that have a traditional pedigree, I have learned the design concepts that are essential to shaping a vision for a new old house. These eight *Pillars of Traditional Design* are the basic building blocks that guide the design of an authentic traditional home with true historic roots.

THE PILLARS OF TRADITIONAL DESIGN

PILLAR ONE

INVENT WITHIN THE RULES

The language of every traditional style—whether Pueblo adobe, Spanish Colonial, Greek Revival, or Craftsman—is recorded in a common set of rules that have guided the designs of generations of builders. These rules are tools that shape the outline of the house, govern the appropriate materials to use, and determine the way the details go together.

Designing a new house using a traditional style is not simply the act of copying from the past. While the historic shapes, building materials, and decorative

In this 1830s Greek Revival farmhouse, the trim around the doors and windows was nailed in place before the drywall installation, imitating the mid-nineteenth-century method of plastering the walls after putting up the trim.

EIGHT PILLARS OF

The Pillars offer a guide to designing a new old house with strong traditional bones. Throughout

PILLAR ONE
INVENT WITHIN THE RULES
Create new designs within the rules of a style; invent with the traditional language of architecture.

PILLAR TWO
RESPECT THE CHARACTER OF PLACE
Fit into the natural character of a place; complement the lay of the land; honor the local building traditions.

PILLAR THREE
TELL A STORY OVER TIME
Script a story about growth over time; imagine changes made by alterations and additions.

PILLAR FOUR
BUILD FOR THE AGES
Build with durable materials and time-tested construction techniques that are sound, sturdy, and built to last.

TRADITIONAL DESIGN

the book, we'll explore the ways architects use these Pillars to create new houses.

PILLAR FIVE

DETAIL FOR AUTHENTICITY

Define house character with authentic details;
make convincing and familiar forms.

PILLAR SIX

CRAFT WITH NATURAL MATERIALS

Build integrity with fine craftsmanship featuring the
timeless beauty of natural materials.

PILLAR SEVEN

CREATE THE PATINA OF AGE

Age by natural weathering processes; build with salvaged
antique materials.

PILLAR EIGHT

INCORPORATE MODERN CONVENIENCES

Integrate modern room functions but hide new
technologies.

An authentic traditional house follows the rules of style. The sturdy columns of this new Southern plantation are taken from history books.

details of old houses can be studied to find out what makes them work, it is possible to be creative with classic style. Ideas for new designs spring from the rules of tradition. Inventing within the rules builds fresh ideas that push traditional forms in a new direction.

PILLAR TWO
RESPECT THE CHARACTER OF PLACE

A new traditional house complements its setting by respecting the character of the place in which it is built. By working with the natural features of the land and by fitting into the distinctive pattern of the neighborhood, a new house can blend into its setting and appear to belong there.

Old-time builders chose house sites that were protected from the weather by topography, sheltered by trees, and close to natural attributes like a hill or pond. An ideal site is one where the house will settle into the lay of the land rather than be perched up on display. A natural saddle of ground where there is a mature stand of trees serves as a backdrop for the house, and it anchors the house in its surroundings, as if it had always been there.

PILLAR THREE
TELL A STORY OVER TIME

Part of the charm of an old house is that it tells a tale of changes over time. In a new house, it is possible to script a story of growth over many years—a room that was remodeled, a wing that was added, or a screen porch that was glassed in—portraying the house as an accumulation of additions.

There can be a storyboard, or a scene-by-scene description, of the history of the house. A new house acquires the soul of the past when it tells a story that covers its newly minted form in a mantle of make-believe.

A classic house is meant to last. Every construction detail should be a testament to its solid permanence and built with solid materials that will stand the test of time, like the stout tapered posts and rugged brackets on the porch of this Craftsman bungalow.

A new house acquires the soul of the past when it tells a story that covers its newly minted form in a mantle of make-believe.

PILLAR FOUR
BUILD FOR THE AGES

Most old houses were made of rugged materials that have withstood the test of time. Poor-quality materials make even a well-designed new house look fragile and inauthentic. A carefully executed traditional house is solid and meant to last—from the masonry foundations to the hardware and interior moldings.

Build a traditional house with long-lasting materials and time-tested construction techniques. There are no substitutes for clapboard siding, stick-built roof rafters, solid-wood doors, and windows with true-divided panes. These sturdy materials are expensive initially, but they pay for themselves in building character and durability for the long run.

PILLAR FIVE
DETAIL FOR AUTHENTICITY

The success of a new old house depends on incorporating details that look familiar and true to form. Details like the shape of the roof, type of windows, molding profiles, and finish materials will look best if they follow historic patterns. The characteristics of a traditional style can be faithfully reproduced from pattern books. Period houses and living-history museums also provide powerful clues about what to build, how historic parts fit together, and how they are used in their proper places to fashion an authentic home.

This new Southern Piedmont farmhouse is often mistaken for a restored historic house.

PILLAR SIX
CRAFT WITH NATURAL MATERIALS

Natural building materials like wood and stone have an organic beauty that cannot be reproduced by synthetic substitutes. Fieldstone walls, wood clapboards, and heart pine floors have surface textures that are rich and warm; but synthetic materials such as vinyl siding and plastic laminate look homogenized, cold, and lifeless. Painstaking craftsmanship with natural materials should be worked into every detail, from the tight fit of a stone wall to the crisp joinery of a mitered door frame.

PILLAR SEVEN
CREATE THE PATINA OF AGE

The distinctive patina of age that burnishes an old house to a mellow vintage can be reproduced by letting nature take its course on a well-chosen selection of new natural materials. Wind and weather will buff a wall of painted clapboard to a satin sheen. And the colors of handmade brick or stone will mute into earth tones after years of rain and mildew work their magic.

By incorporating antique building parts into the construction, a new house looks old from the beginning because it is built with materials that have a time-worn natural patina of instant credibility. Salvaged building parts—such as doors, mantelpieces, and light fixtures—preserve a bit of history tempered by time. Recycled pine floors and antique doorknobs reveal marks of wear from years of handling that are telltale signs of their past.

PILLAR EIGHT
INCORPORATE MODERN CONVENIENCES

Most of the essential creature comforts of modern living can be woven into the fabric of a traditional house without being intrusive or overwhelming. New functions that never existed in old houses— bathrooms with indoor plumbing, eat-in kitchens, family rooms, laundries, and home offices—can be integrated into the layout of a traditional floor plan by rearranging the pattern of rooms.

Like the history of many Midwestern farmhouses, the story of this prairie home is told in rambling additions that appear to have grown over many decades. A new house can mimic a home with a past when it is designed with fictional additions.

Antique houses have influenced each home shown in this book. The new farmhouse above is a historic house that was reconstructed by moving many of the parts from Connecticut to Maryland. The house features the stylistic details of Georgian architecture from the eighteenth century, such as a portico with a pedimented roof and two-story fluted pilaster columns on the outside corners of the facade.

Genuine details give familiar form to a traditional style. Handmade terra-cotta roof tiles and walls of rough-cast stucco are the hallmarks of authenticity on a new Spanish Colonial home. These elements of historic detail faithfully reproduce the character of this architectural classic.

New technical innovations—such as the heating and air-conditioning systems, computer networks, security detectors, and televisions—can be concealed within the structure of the house. Most of these systems can be inserted into the framing without intruding on the finish work. Special features such as control panels can be hidden in wall cabinets, behind grilles, or within secret compartments. Seamlessly weaving these conveniences into the house during the planning stage preserves the ambiance of the old by integrating the new with craft and ingenuity.

HOW THE PILLARS OF TRADITIONAL DESIGN WORK

The Pillars of Traditional Design epitomize the design intuition, handcraftsmanship, and time-honored building practices inherited from Old World builders. These eight Pillars organize a way of thinking about how to translate traditional values into a new home.

The Pillars are presented in an order that represents the natural design process. The benefits are cumulative, because the results of using one Pillar builds on what is learned from using the one before it. Once the rules of a traditional style are understood, a new design can be invented that respects the character of place and tells a story over time. Then it is possible to build for the ages using authentic details that are crafted with natural materials and seasoned with the patina of age. Finally, by incorporating modern conveniences, a new old house will work well for today's lifestyle.

The Pillars are universal guidelines that anyone can use as tools to recreate a real traditional home. These are traditional skills, recovered from our ancestors, and known as "the old way of building."

Natural materials, like these cedar shingle walls and granite foundations, impart an organic beauty to the finished character of a new old house.

In true colonial revival fashion, details of the stair are classically inspired, such as the Georgian handrail and balusters, which descend in a curve and coil into a tight volute.

THE OLD WAY OF BUILDING

Most traditional American house styles were originally used for simple farmhouses and evolved into mature forms over hundreds of years. From place to place, there developed a remarkably rich texture to the regional traditions of house building. Regional styles took root in American soil from the seeds of many Old World cultures imported with the first settlers. Distinctive details and techniques for fashioning materials expressed the unique craft traditions of builders from different backgrounds. Slowly, styles evolved that were adapted to the geography and climate of each region of the country—the Southwest adobe, the New England saltbox, the Southern Tidewater plantation, the Louisiana Creole cottage. Over

The creature comforts of technology and the necessities of modern family living are seamlessly incorporated into the design of this new old house. Functional equipment concealed within the walls, with new reproduction fixtures, complement the period interior decor.

A home built for the ages recalls the hallmarks of old-time craftsmanship expressed in durable materials shaped by caring hands.

time, these styles matured into the distinctly American forms of old houses that we know today.

In times past, master builders designed houses by following the inherited traditions and collective building wisdom of their ancestors—principles commonly accepted then as the old way of building. Traditional building patterns were passed on from one generation to the next through carpenters and craftsmen, who erected fine houses simply by following the rules of thumb.

The old-time builders made houses that were well crafted, harmonious, and workable. They understood the basic principles of composition, material, and detail, in time-honored building practices. I incorporated the lessons I learned from the old way of building into the eight Pillars of Traditional Design.

Today, practical guidelines can help us recapture the practices that were so intuitive to the master builders of the past. With the Pillars in mind, we can build new houses that are as connected to place, as well crafted, and as harmonious as old houses.

THE FAUX TRADITIONAL HOUSE: A HOUSE MEANT FOR CURB APPEAL

Many of today's homebuilders seem to have lost touch with the principles of the old way of building. Keenly aware of the attraction of old architectural styles, the faux traditional house has become universal in subdivisions across the country. These

are houses built with a veneer of history pasted onto the surface like wallpaper. Contemporary homebuilders on tight timetables tend to shun the old way of building, because it requires a commitment to craft and quality. But the result is the placeless and confusing suburban house that is cobbled together into a design stew.

When we see a faux traditional home, most of us recognize instinctively that something about the house is wrong. Without good composition, proportion, and craftsmanship, the results are clumsy and confusing to the eye. The front facade is a billboard mockup of tradition, and the backside is a hodge-podge of randomly placed windows, odd bump-

The features of modern convenience should be carefully woven into a traditional house. Here, turn-of-the-century cabinets, hardware, and lighting fixtures blend with state-of-the-art appliances.

A traditional house is crafted with natural materials—such as wood clapboard, or fieldstone—that are durable and well composed, blending craftsmanship and proportion. The interplay of these handcrafted details gives a traditional house its rich texture and harmonious design.

CRAFTING YOUR OWN CLASSIC HOME

This book features new houses that honor the traditional virtues of the old way of building. Through photographs and words, with brief digressions into history and craftsmanship and occasional sidelong glances at the inner workings of real old houses, a story emerges about how traditional houses go together and what gives them their unique design appeal. The architectural details and hallmarks of style that are distinctive to the home's tradition will be highlighted throughout each house profile.

Each house chosen for the book is one of the best examples of a traditional regional style from across the country, selected from hundreds of homes designed by the finest architects and builders. These design professionals and homeowners from all corners of America are tapping into our rich heritage of building styles. This book uncovers the challenges and creative solutions behind building the best new traditional houses by giving fresh treatment to historic styles and by reinterpreting the classics with amenities that suit the way homeowners live today.

outs, and jutting roofs. The mass-produced decorative details look tentative and impermanent. We recognize that they are houses built for expediency and not for beauty, and they were never meant to last.

THE NEW OLD HOUSE: A HOME MEANT TO LAST

A real traditional home is rooted in the landscape, conceived with familiar forms and harmonious details, crafted by caring hands, and planned for comfort. Whereas a faux traditional house has a haphazard veneer of historic styles, a new old house has integrity built on simple forms and graceful lines.

The appearance of a traditional home is familiar, reminding us of places we have seen before, conjuring memories of houses that have a recognizable character. Unlike the faux traditional house for which the land is contorted into a convenient building platform, a real traditional house is intimately connected with its setting, as if it grew naturally from the contours of the land.

A pair of sash-and-panel doors built of antique cypress open into the front entrance hall of this recreation of a French colonial plantation house.

A COTTAGE ON THE COAST

SPANISH CARIBBEAN COLONIAL

An arcade of stucco arches raises the open veranda of the Spanish Caribbean cottage. The design blends the traditions of Florida's Spanish colonial era (1565–1763) with the raised plantation houses of the West Indies and the tin-roofed Cracker cottages of nineteenth-century Florida.

When Norman and Cindi Mansour decided to build on the shore of Anna Maria Island, they knew what they did not want: a beach house propped up on spindly wooden stilts. Instead, they wanted a sturdy, durable home inspired by the traditions of Florida architecture.

BLENDING HISTORIC STYLES

The house that architect Don Cooper designed for the Mansours is an ingenious blend of seventeenth-century Spanish Colonial arches and nineteenth-century Florida Cracker tin roofs. The architect decided to *Invent within the Rules* by drawing on details of two historic styles to create a new design that preserves traces of both traditions. From the stout arcade of Spanish arches to the airy Caribbean veranda and delicate Cracker

dormers, each aspect of the house is *Detailed for Authenticity* to reproduce genuine character. The sturdy masonry foundations covered in stucco and the braced-frame tin roof are *Built for the Ages* to withstand the ravages of Gulf storms. Inside, the rooms are arranged to *Incorporate Modern Conveniences*; spaces are organized in the patterns of modern living, and the mechanics of technology are integrated within the walls.

The Mansours combed the Gulf Coast, searching for historic inspiration for their new house and found treasures on the old-fashioned resort island of Boca Grande. The Gasparilla Island Lighthouse of 1890 suggested the concept of a square floor plan with wraparound porches under a hipped roof supported by square columns. And the colonnade of Spanish colonial arches and heavy masonry piers on the old Railway Depot, built in 1910, provided a way to avoid wooden stilts for the foundation.

Don put the ground-floor arcade of the railway depot together with the raised porch and square columns of the lighthouse to form a Spanish Caribbean raised cottage that is sheltered under a pavilion-style tin roof. The new design makes a perfect pairing of historic themes and *Respects the Character of Place* by fitting in and becoming a landmark on tropical Anna Maria Island.

The architect decided to invent within classic rules by drawing on details of two historic styles to create a new design that preserves traces of both traditions.

Above left: The sturdy foundation arches, made of stucco on concrete block with a wood frame, are modeled after the arcades of the Spanish Revival railway depot on Boca Grande Island.

Above right: Typical of a raised Caribbean cottage, a covered veranda wraps around the main living floor, opening the house to cooling sea breezes while shielding it from the sun. Square wood posts carry the overhanging roof, with pairs of dark green plantation shutters framing the oversize windows.

Right: A pair of West Indies–style French doors open into the entry hall. Recessed flat panels and hardwood floors convey the formal simplicity of a colonial plantation house.

RECAPTURING
THE ROMANCE OF
SPAIN

Architect Thomas Bollay's own romantic Spanish Colonial Revival home blends the traditional architecture of rural Spain with the Mediterranean-style houses of 1920s California. These traditions are fused in an authentic revival of Spanish forms. From the style of the *casa del campo*—the typical farmhouse of the Spanish countryside—come rough-cast stucco walls and red tile roofs.

An outdoor fireplace and grille provide a romantic focal point for the brick dining patio. Coarsely textured stucco walls are reminiscent of a typical rural Spanish casa del campo. The wrought-iron balcony is another picturesque Spanish detail, added for authenticity.

The outdoor stone staircase coils around the tower, emphasizing its curving form.

Thomas, an architect, designed his home in the lush foothills of Montecito, keeping three Pillars of Traditional Design in mind. First, the house *Respects the Character of Place,* fitting snugly into the landscape so it looks as if the grove of ancient oaks and eucalyptus trees had matured around it over the past hundred years. Second, the house is *Crafted with Natural Materials* to give the home its tactile beauty. Finally, by recreating *Details of Authenticity*, such as the wrought-iron balconies, the house is faithful to the historic style of the Spanish Colonial Revival. All of the elements are handled with simplicity and restraint, a key lesson in creating a new old house.

Peaking through the oak tree at the left is the short tower that is the elbow of the pinwheel floor plan. Located next to the tower is a wooden balcony, lime washed to look aged.

The timber balcony outside the second-story master bedroom is a Spanish detail adapted from the colonial townhouses of Monterey that were built when Spanish missionaries settled the California coast in the eighteenth century.

hallmarks of style
THE SPANISH COLONIAL REVIVAL IN CALIFORNIA

Architects in southern California created the Spanish Colonial Revival style in the 1920s as a way to promote the eighteenth-century Spanish roots of the region. The style reinterpreted the early houses of coastal California and the provincial architecture of rural Spain from the fifteenth century in houses with low-pitched roofs, red barrel-shaped roof tiles, stucco walls, and arched windows with ornamental wrought-iron accents. Details were also freely adapted from Mexico and a variety of Mediterranean traditions, particularly Italian, to produce houses that were an eclectic mix of styles with floor plans tailored to modern needs.

Thomas Bollay designed Casa de la Torre by studying his large collection of working drawings from leading architects of the 1920s, paying particular attention to plans by George Washington Smith, the master of the Spanish Colonial Revival style in Santa Barbara.

The front of the house resembles a casa del campo, *a provincial farmhouse from rural Spain, tucked into an ancient grove of oaks and eucalyptus.*

A TIMELESS TOWER

A traditional Spanish tower, diminutive in size, peeks through the treetops. The shallow cone of the tower's roof, covered in mission tiles, is a play on the authentic traditions of Spain. Towers were a favorite theme of the Spanish Colonial Revival architects of the early twentieth century, although they were seldom part of rural Spanish farmhouses. The house derives its name, Casa de la Torre, from this tower, which rises through the middle of the house and joins the wings of the home.

A THRESHOLD WITH HISTORY
The simplicity and restraint of provincial Spanish architecture is captured in the front doorway of Casa de la Torre. The classical portico is a simply detailed front door surround made of square stucco pilaster

The entry hall staircase looks like stone, but it is wood covered in plaster. The floors are tiled in a traditional basket-weave pattern, with Spanish decorative inserts. The wrought-iron doors were rescued from the Santa Barbara Biltmore Hotel.

➤ The house wouldn't be fully authentic if the architect relied only on antique architectural details to create a period Mediterranean home. The playfulness and variety of the tilework also clearly identify the interior of this newly built house as Spanish in origin. Tile, an inexpensive handicraft material and cool to the touch, was commonly used in old-fashioned Spanish houses for floors, wainscoting wall panels, and stairs. More often than not, the floor tiles were plain terra-cotta slabs, whereas walls were decorated with hand-painted tiles in exuberant patterns, called *azulejos*. On the floor of the tiled entry vestibule and stair hall of Casa de la Torre, unglazed terra-cotta tiles are set in a basket-weave pattern that is studded with decorative glazed earthenware tiles, called *olambrillas*.

The imported glazed cobalt blue azulejos tiles in the bath look like the glazed earthenware tiles commonly used for decorative surfaces in old Spanish houses.

columns that support a plain frieze, or horizontal beam, and a cornice. The Spanish cedar front door, framed inside the surround, is made of vertical wooden planks studded with iron rosette-head nails. Above the portico, a handcrafted wrought-iron balconet, or miniature balcony, is mounted outside a pair of second-story French doors. This collection of shapes and textures draws the eye to the door as the centerpiece of the facade.

Inside the arch of the front doorway hangs a pair of antique iron doors, wrought in a fretwork of twisted spindles, salvaged from renovations to the Mediterranean-style Santa Barbara Biltmore Hotel (built in 1926). Open-work wrought-iron doors were used in old-fashioned Spanish houses to promote air circulation while keeping the interior of the house secure. The vintage door grilles further authenticate the house with pieces of history.

EXTENDING THE LIVING SPACE

Once inside the vestibule, rooms that go off in unexpected directions make it clear that the floor plan is unlike any other new house. Because the plan is arranged as wings attached in a pinwheel pattern around the central tower, the major rooms in the house don't align at right angles. Since the wings are only one room deep, both the living room and the dining room are open to the outdoors on two sides to allow for cross ventilation through pairs of French doors on opposite walls.

Another reason for the unique plan is that the architect wanted to angle the rooms to take best advantage of natural views and access to the gardens. In one wing, the living room and master bedroom have north views to the Santa Ynez Mountains. In another, the kitchen and dining room open onto a brick-paved patio, terraced above the gardens on axis with a future pool, a way to enjoy the outdoor lifestyle prevalent in Santa Barbara. The least important part of the house, the garage, faces away from the best views.

COLORFUL SPANISH TILES

The centerpiece of the entry hall is the tiled staircase, its sculptural form vividly patterned with a unique row of hand-painted ceramic tiles on each

A PINWHEEL PLAN

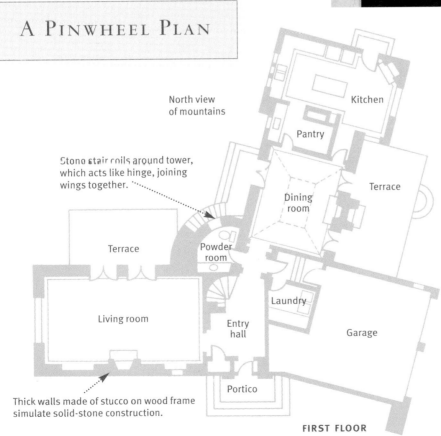

North view of mountains

Stone stair coils around tower, which acts like hinge, joining wings together.

Kitchen

Pantry

Dining room

Terrace

Terrace

Powder room

Laundry

Living room

Entry hall

Garage

Thick walls made of stucco on wood frame simulate solid-stone construction.

Portico

FIRST FLOOR

The view through the hallway to the dining room reveals the thickened walls of double archways that simulate heavy plastered stone. Two steps of terra-cotta tiles create a transition from one room to the next.

Mediterranean-style tiles and furnishings, paired with whitewashed walls, help replicate an old Spanish Revival—style home.

The dining room's tray ceiling beams are made of lime-washed Douglas fir and feature a wooden Moorish star pattern set into each beam. The terra-cotta tiled floor was treated with linseed oil and carnauba wax to create a rich patina that will deepen with time.

riser. The fluidly curved staircase, with its hammered iron handrail, arcs its way up to the second-floor bedroom landing. Like an old Spanish stair made of solid masonry, the vaulted arch of the wooden stair carriage is finished in plaster to look like stone. The curved shape of the stair is a reminder that it is in the inside curve of Casa de la Torre's tower. Mediterranean-style tiles and furnishings, paired with whitewashed walls, help replicate an old Spanish Revival—style home.

The hallway from the stairs into the dining room is skewed at a soft angle that reflects the unique geometry of the floor plan. Filled with southern sunlight, the dining room's tray ceiling, made of whitewashed Douglas fir beams, glows with illumination. A pair of double tie-beams spans the width of the room and are decorated with an inlaid pattern of wooden Moorish stars that were a favorite motif of architect George Washington Smith, the master of the 1920s Spanish Colonial Revival movement in California.

On the floor, unglazed terra-cotta tiles, arranged in a field-and-border pattern using two shades of red, have a charming, aged luster from being hand-polished with linseed oil and carnauba wax.

SIMULATING STONE IN PLASTER AND WOOD

In centuries past, the walls of rural Spanish farmhouses were built of rough fieldstone covered with stucco and painted with a whitewash of lime paste. The walls were often several feet thick, with plain openings for doors and windows, which were set deep into the wall for protection from the weather.

One of the hallmarks of a Spanish Colonial Revival house is a stucco-finished wall. But solid-stone wall construction is prohibitively expensive today and doesn't comply with earthquake-resistance building codes in California. So architect Thomas Bollay came up with a way to make his house look like stone.

A MODERN SOLUTION His solution was to build the walls with two layers of wood studs to create a wall with a hollow cavity in the middle but built out to the thickness of stone. Covered in rough-cast stucco, the cavity in the 2-ft.-thick wall is used to run ductwork, plumbing, and electrical wires everywhere in the house. To add another dimension to the convincing look of stone, the windows and doors are deeply recessed into the center of the wall thickness. Set back 1 ft. into the stucco exterior walls, the window wells create deep shadows. Rounded stucco jambs and window sills simulate the look of stone.

The walls of rural Spanish fieldstone farmhouses had a rough texture. The modern way to give stucco a rough-cast look is to slather the stucco plaster on the walls in coarse layers, rather than in smooth strokes. Creating a wall of bumps and pockets in plaster simulates the look of aged stucco over stone walls. Stucco is a pliable material that can create sculptural effects. After the plaster has set, the walls are painted bright white to imitate the appearance of whitewash. This technique can be used for exterior and interior walls for a heavy, rustic texture.

A robust living room fireplace, with a 4-ft.-wide hearth opening commands attention. The stout proportions of the plastered mantel give the room an exaggerated Old World air.

MAKING IMPERFECT MISSION TILES

➤ Part of the charm of an early Spanish house lies in its imperfect rustic roof tiles. On old Spanish tile roofs, the barrel-shaped clay tiles, called mission tiles, were made by hand over curved

wood molds and baked in the sun to harden. As a result of forming and curing one tile at a time, the tiles were irregular in shape. When stacked on a roof, they look distinctly uneven or crooked.

The architect found that today's machine-pressed Spanish tiles were too precisely manufactured and uniform in shape for his house. A local tile maker cast each roof tile by hand in the classic barrel-arch shape. The terra-cotta tiles were then installed in an intentionally irregular pattern, with uneven heights and staggered edges to exaggerate the handcrafted character of the roof. The tiles are now sold locally, where they are known as the "Bollay" tile.

OLD WORLD CHARACTER BLENDS WITH MODERN

On the other side of the stair hall, the living room feels taller because it is down a few steps. A modern-style steel and glass studio window fills the far end of the room, offering a vista of ancient oaks. The grand scale of the room is underscored by a robust fireplace, which dominates the long wall. The over-scaled fireplace coupled with the heavy wood beams on the ceiling imprint the room with a sturdy Old World character. The fireplace is traditional Spanish style, with a plaster surround and a hood that tapers into the ceiling. Across from the hearth, two pairs of French doors again join the interiors to the garden, completing the circle of living indoors and out.

A small roof, piled with thick tile and propped up on wrought-iron S-brackets, covers the back door.

The oversize modern-style window draws the eye to the gnarled silhouette of an ancient oak. The writing table and chair are reproduction Spanish Colonial Revival pieces of the 1920s, purchased when the Santa Barbara Biltmore Hotel was renovated.

RIVER HOUSE
IN BIG SKY COUNTRY

This old cattle ranch is found in the hills of western Montana, where ranching has been a way of life since Midwesterners settled the high plains in the 1860s. The ranch was a ramshackle legacy of buildings from the turn of the last century that included a plain ranch-style house along with calving sheds, a few log barns, a tin wagon shed, and smaller outbuildings.

Outbuildings on the old ranch were reconstructed for new uses. The old ice-house was redesigned to store fishing tackle, and the reconstructed horse barn, located beyond the farm bell, now houses a game room and bunk house.

The ranch house, seen through the classic western gallows gate, is a notched log cabin in the Rocky Mountain rustic style. The cabin is one and a half stories, with the traditional low eaves and simple shingled gable roof typical of the style.

Although the place was time worn, the homeowner saw promise in the forlorn-looking property and asked architects Bill Curtis and Russell Windham to coax the motley group of buildings into a working ranch, while preserving its Montana roots. The existing ranch house was an unremarkable log structure, dating back to the late 1890s with little more than an empty shell worth saving. But the place was perfectly located next to a world-class trout stream. Bill and Russell rebuilt the entire house from the ground up to create a more authentic version of the pioneer log cabins that were built here by ranchers in the late nineteenth century.

The trick was to turn a plain house into a period cabin fitted out with historic details that improved on the original design, without becoming theatrical, and that made the ranch house look and feel genuine and vintage.

The architects began by studying the character of the houses in surrounding valleys and the building traditions that shaped them, so that their new design would fit in with the old local ranch architecture of the area. Their inspiration came from the local vernacular of simple log ranch houses and barns built before 1900, along with images of the Rocky Mountain lodges of our national parks.

The reconstructed cabin uses the traditional details of notched log construction, like crossed corners and overhanging log roof rafters. The architectural details, coupled with the up-to-date structural and mechanical systems, make the rebuilt house both functional and *Built for the Ages.*

Inside the ranch, new finishes are rendered to look old. Artisans used painted finishes and distressing techniques to make the rebuilt house look tarnished by wear, *Creating the Patina of Age* without crossing the line into cowboy kitsch. The new old house is successful because it avoids clichés and is just plain comfortable, like a well-worn pair of jeans.

BUILDING WITH LOGS

The western ranchers imported their basic knowledge of log construction from the frontier east, where pioneers who settled the Appalachian Mountains of Virginia, Kentucky, and Tennessee mastered

The connected row of double-hung windows dates the porch to the turn of the twentieth century, while the crossed log corners match the original cabin.

hallmarks of style
ROCKY MOUNTAIN RANCH

he cattle ranch has a long history in western Montana, a place that has provided abundant pastureland for beef cattle since the 1860s, when Midwestern ranchers migrated to the mountain valleys.

With vast forests for timber, the new settlers built almost every structure they needed with logs—houses, barns, work sheds, and fences. Thus the houses they built were four square and simple in plan, dictated by stacking logs to form straight-line boxes. When the house was enlarged, as family needs grew, another log box was added on, extending the length of the house in a telescoping plan.

On the earliest nineteenth-century houses, the roof was made of split logs or rough wood planks that ran from the roof peak to the eaves. These rough roofing boards were later covered with split shingles to make the roof more weather tight. At the turn of the twentieth century, metal roofs were favored when the material was made available with the advent of railroads.

The low 7-ft., 6-in. ceilings of the living room make the space feel intimate, like a one-room cabin. White plaster panels on the ceiling brighten the log room. The fireplace is made of blocks of Colorado moss rock, which fit together precisely and leave the natural weathered faces and moss patches exposed.

log building a century earlier. Early ranch houses are distinguished by the way in which the logs are stacked and finished. Most houses were built with peeled logs left round, though some were built with logs squared on four sides with an ax.

The most distinctive feature of log house construction is the corner joint, where the logs cross each other. This joint varies from simple log construction, where squared-log ends are stacked like bricks and spiked together to elaborate dovetail joints made of interlocking Vs that hold without fasteners. On this new old house, the corner joints are saddle notched and crowned. To make this unusual joint, the builder notches a round pocket, or saddle, out of the end of

each of the logs to form a perfect seat for the log stacked above it. The ends of each of the logs are left overlong so that they stick out at the corners, a technique called crowning.

The space between the logs is usually chinked, or filled in with materials, to make the joint airtight. Traditional chinking was done with small stones, brush, or even torn hopsacks and shredded old blankets. The exterior joint was mortared closed with mud paste, a durable mortar made of lime and sand. On the inside, a small sapling was wedged between each of the logs to make a more pleasing-looking interior finish, a traditional technique that the architects used for this new old house.

A BLEND OF OLD AND NEW PARTS

A rack of antlers, a symbol of old-fashioned pioneer traditions in the Rocky Mountains, is mounted above the front door as a welcoming gesture. The single-story ranch house is built of logs of lodgepole pine, which were probably harvested from the nearby mountainside. Like many late-nineteenth-century settlers' cabins in the high valley, the log walls are notched and crossed at the corners.

A new foundation under the house provides a firm footing and basement space, which *Incorporates the Modern Conveniences* of heating, electricity, and water supply. The old peeled logs stack on top of new foundation walls, covered with smooth river stones that were pulled from the stream bed behind the house. A stout stone chimney is built of the same stones, which have been tumbled round by the river. Because the building materials were drawn from the nearby landscape, the house feels like a part of the setting and complements the land.

The restored logs are stained with a solid brown pigment that makes the walls look brand new, highlighted by the bright white chinking of the fresh mortar. And the new split cedar shingles on the roof have not yet weathered to their dusty gray patina. But time and weather will soften the raw new look to *Create the Patina of Age* by bleaching the colors and by staining the mortar with character.

A TELESCOPING CABIN PLAN

A small bedroom wing, added to the ranch house in the 1950s by previous owners, telescopes off one end of the main cabin, in the same way that log houses were extended historically. A new breakfast room porch was added to the river side of the

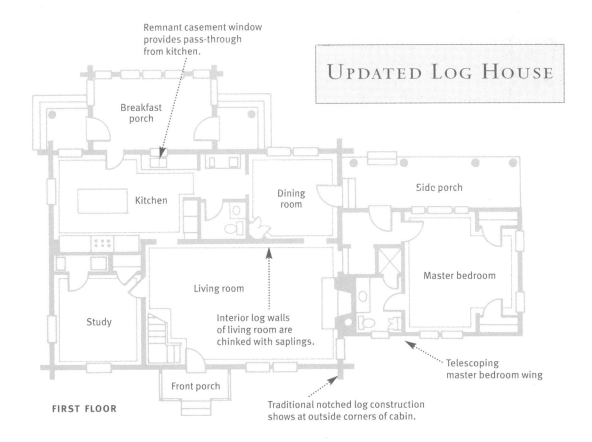

Remnant casement window provides pass-through from kitchen.

Breakfast porch

UPDATED LOG HOUSE

Kitchen

Dining room

Side porch

Master bedroom

Living room

Interior log walls of living room are chinked with saplings.

Study

Telescoping master bedroom wing

Front porch

Traditional notched log construction shows at outside corners of cabin.

FIRST FLOOR

The rustic open staircase inside the front door is made of hand-hewn timbers and thick plank treads supported by a log bracket.

house, enclosed on three sides by a band of sash windows that can be opened to the sounds and scents of the water. Built of logs and river stones that duplicate the original cabin, this small addition fits naturally with the traditional architecture of the place but adds a new type of indoor–outdoor room that was unknown in the pioneer days.

A PERSUASIVE PATINA

Architects and artisans worked together to *Create the Patina of Age* on the interiors. The illusion of age begins at the front door, where the living room persuades visitors that the cabin is at least a century old. The designers blended faux finishes and antique building materials into the rebuilt house for the look of an old mountain lodge.

The amber wood walls of the living room feel like those of an old fishing cabin, hung with artwork and memorabilia collected over a lifetime. Four walls are lined with half-round peeled logs that have been stained and varnished to create a mellow color. Log beams crisscross the low ceiling between panels of textured plaster and seem to compress the room, making it cozy. The floors are made of salvaged oak resawn into wide floorboards of random widths.

MOUNTAIN LODGE FINISHES

An open staircase made of hewn timbers fills the inside corner of the living room. The stair carriage is made of stout beams and wood plank treads that have been hand-finished with an adz, a hoe-like ax with a curved blade, for a rustic effect. Each of the handrail pickets is a slat of hewn wood with the bark edges left on. These textured finishes are blackened and stained to a caramel color to turn the new wood into a convincing antique, an aging technique that can be applied to any woodwork.

At the far end of the living room, architects Bill and Russell created a craggy stone fireplace made of Colorado ledgestone, which was inspired by the style of early national park lodges. Many of the stones are covered with moss and lichen, left on at the quarry, which is sometimes called moss rock. Stacked in a dry-laid pattern, without any visible mortar joints, the rough-block stonework looks finely tailored. The mason's art shows in the subtle fitting of one stone to the next and in the massive lintel that spans across the fireplace. In early mountain cabins, these hefty stone fireplaces were often

Walls in the dining room are horizontal 1x8 flush boards painted celery white to contrast with the dark-stained beadboard ceiling. The palette of finishes is simple and rustic, but Crafted with Natural Materials *that make the room feel tailored.*

Barns and Outbuildings

Most of the calving sheds on the original cattle ranch were torn down, but the wagon shed was rebuilt. The new ranch compound includes the renovated old horse barn and the old blacksmith's shop, now used to house equipment.

A working western cattle ranch would not be complete without a full complement of barns and outbuildings. Among the existing buildings on the ranch that were saved, the old blacksmith's shop and horse barn have been restored. The horse barn, built at the turn of the last century, is a classic western-style two-story barn made of hewn logs with a timber-frame hayloft above the ground-floor horse stalls. But the barn has been refitted as a game room and guest quarters with a homespun cowboy character.

Top right: **The hewn timber rafters and king post trusses above the game room in the barn are new and added for decorative effect.** Roughsawn roofing boards and wall panels more closely resemble traditional barn finishes.

Bottom right: **The bunkhouse is a classic ranch hands' quarters, gussied up to be a guest bedroom.** The peeled-log ceiling beams are original, and new walls and floors are left unfinished to add rustic character.

The hayloft is a soaring game room and bar dressed up in early western style. The walls and floors are finished with new roughsawn planks, and the ceiling timbers are heavy hewn beams that are both decorative and structural, inserted under the old roof frame. Furnished with leather chairs and Native American rugs, the rusticity of the room plays up the cowboy theme done in the high style of the New West.

The Old West is preserved in the guest bedroom, which is housed in a part of the horse barn that was once a granary. This room was made to look like an updated version of a wranglers' bunkhouse. The iron bed frames and reproduction nineteenth-century drop-cord lights dress the room with *Details for Authenticity*.

INSTANT TARNISHED INTERIORS

Patina is the tarnished appearance that a material takes on through years of exposure or wear, like the rich brown of an old copper penny or the hand-rubbed luster on a well-used doorknob. In a new old house, the patina of age can be introduced instantly, but it is a process of surface finishing that requires artistic skill.

A Santa Fe artist who specializes in faux finishes created the palette of distressed finishes throughout this ranch. By subtly grading paint and stain tones, the artist coaxed time-worn effects from shiny new surfaces. The grooves between boards are blackened as if embedded with dirt, the wall colors are smoked as if the paint had faded unevenly, and the cabinet finishes are rubbed thin as if handled by generations. The finishes were applied in layers, from a base coat of pure color to the darkening tones that were streaked over it. Where the finish is to look worn, the paint is wiped off or spot sanded down to bare wood.

The mustard yellow basecoat on the bathroom vanity was aged by unevenly ragging dark stain over the surface and into the joints of the boards.

made with round river stones, another way to tie the interiors to the rustic landscape outdoors.

The key to creating the mystique of the Old West inside the cabin came from a blend of antique materials and faux finishes. Faux finishing gives the kitchen an old-fashioned aura. Old oak floorboards and the beadboard ceiling are stained a deep scotch brown. The walls are made of wood boards, painted and then ragged with a smoky stain to make them look faded by time.

Newly minted kitchen cabinets are designed of simple plank frames with beaded panel doors. The cabinets are made to look well worn by the addition of old-fashioned bin pulls and butt hinges. The woodwork was aged by painting it a muddy celery white and then rubbing it down to bare wood in many places to create wear marks.

The new breakfast room porch, built to replace the old porch, looks out to the creek. When the architects added on the new room, they left a casement window in the wall to provide a pass-through to the kitchen. New saddle-notched logs are used for the walls and ceiling beams, making this room look like the rest of the cabin. Notches leftover from old roof rafters leave traces of earlier construction, so the cabin *Tells a Story Over Time.*

From the breakfast porch, the kitchen is visible beyond a pass-through created by a casement window that was leftover when the porch was added on. A notched log across the top of the wall suggests places where old rafters were once set into the wall.

REVIVING A
PRIMITIVE
POWER

Intrigued by the traditional techniques of adobe construction, architect Michael Bauer crafted a house with baked mud walls and timber beams to create a new adobe with an interior that is *Invented within the Rules* of the style. Almost nothing in this adobe is faked, except for the modern weatherproof finishes.

The kitchen of this adobe house has a ceiling shaped in long plastered coves, or barrel vaults, that rest on top of log vigas. This type of ceiling was most likely introduced by the Spanish, because the local native peoples had no experience with vaulted construction.

PUEBLO ADOBE ARCHITECTURE

Adobe is the simplest of ancient building crafts, developed by Pueblo Indians more than 1,000 years ago. Although adobe is often used to describe an architectural style, it is actually a building material. Adobe houses are made of thick mud walls that absorb heat during the day, keeping interiors cool, and radiate heat at night, keeping interiors warm. Sun-baked bricks of clay earth dug from the ground and molded by hand are stacked into walls that are held together by adobe mortar and covered with coats of hand-smoothed mud plaster.

Primitive adobe bricks had little compressive strength, and rains eroded the mud finish. After the rains, adobe mud was drawn from the ground back up the walls to rebuild them.

Spanish missionaries who settled the Southwest throughout the 1800s adapted and refined the native adobe buildings by adding framed doors, casement windows, and covered porches. The adobe architecture of Santa Fe is a hybrid of Pueblo mud brick walls ornamented with a lacework of wooden posts and beams derived from Spanish traditions.

The new house is traditional adobe construction. The walls are made of solid adobe bricks, the roof is supported by hand-hewn beams and round log *vigas*, and wooden lintels carry the heavy adobe over windows and doors. The plain and unadorned adobe walls are 1 ft. to 2 ft. thick, covered with an undulating surface of sand-textured stucco smoothed by hand in traditional soft profiles.

There are no modern construction necessities that compromise tradition, such as concealed bearing walls, hidden steel beams, or covered roof trusses. But the house's authenticity is tempered with practical convenience by rethinking the simple adobe floor plan to accommodate the complex needs of a modern household.

Though this adobe looks antique from the outside, inside, it functions like a modern home in ways that were never imagined in ancient times. Many small building blocks are joined together to form a house with the rambling character of a Pueblo village, enclosing contemporary spaces for living, dining, kitchen, and baths.

The guesthouse is an authentic adobe structure on the high point of the property. The small casita, or cottage, is of traditional adobe construction, with simple plastered walls of rose-tan adobe, rounded at the corners in imitation of ancient Native American dwellings built from 900 to 1200.

The house is a rambling collection of adobe building blocks. The informal composition of clustered parts recalls the architecture of traditional Native American village pueblos.

A COLLECTION OF CONNECTING PARTS

Looking much like the early pueblos, or communal American Indian villages of adobe dwellings, this new adobe house is a tightly knit structure of many connected parts. From afar, the house looks like a scattered collection of native adobe building blocks tucked into the mature piñon pines. In ancient pueblo architecture, each part of the house is added on to join the whole. Native adobe houses started as one-room dwellings, with new rooms added as the household grew. The additions were often placed where needed rather than following a formal plan, and rooms were also built one on top of another. This irregular massing is reflected in the unpredictable plan of this new house, where the concept of additions has been used to accommodate the functions of contemporary living.

MODERN ADOBE WALLS

Today, adobe is the ultimate green building material. It is plentiful in supply and energy efficient—cool in summer and warm in winter. Today's adobe bricks are available in two types: *untreated or semistabilized*. Both types are made of mud and dried in the sun in the traditional manner. For durability, the adobe bricks are mortared together with a modern mixture of Portland cement.

Untreated, or *traditional*, bricks are made of a mixture of sand, silt, and clay, with straw added for strength and to prevent cracking. Water is added, and the mixture is tightly packed into wooden brick molds called *adoberos*. After the bricks set, they are removed from the molds and put in the sun to bake for several weeks.

Semistabilized adobe bricks are made with a small amount of asphalt emulsion or cement added to the adobe mixture. The stabilizer gives the bricks a measure of water resistance, which protects them from rain damage during the sun-baking process.

Twin blank walls of adobe form the approach to the house (above). Within the austere walls, a private interior courtyard with an old ponderosa pine in the center is surrounded by the building blocks of the house. Tucked into the thickness of an adobe wall, the front door is made of rough-hewn planks with a delicate wrought-iron grille. Wooden casement windows are set into the walls as if pushed into soft mud, with no trim except for the lintel beams that span across the tops. The only decorative relief on the facade is the carved wooden downspouts, called *canales*, that pierce the walls to drain rainwater from the roof.

Once through the front door, a visitor sees that the entry vestibule is at the intersection of a bright cross hall and the cool half light of the living room.

The cross hall is a sunlit passageway through an arcade of arched openings made of plaster. The stout wooden lintels above thick plaster walls with rounded corners emphasize the solid character of the adobe construction and are a reminder that the house is made of 2-ft.-thick walls.

QUIET PLACES

The new old house has an unpredictable floor plan, like that of an ancient dwelling found in a Pueblo village. The house tumbles downhill in a cluster of adobe blocks that contain the bedrooms, the kitchen and dining room, and finally the living room, which is on the lowest level. The interior rooms are staggered on these different levels throughout the plan.

Stepped adobe walls follow the front stairs down to the front door. A coating of modern inted cement stucco covers the adobe bricks to protect the walls from the weather. Casement windows were introduced into adobe architecture by the Spanish as a useful improvement.

Decorative downspouts, called canales, sit on top of carved bracket supports. Such details are part of the Spanish heritage that began when iron woodworking tools were brought to the Southwest.

PLAN FOR A SLOPE

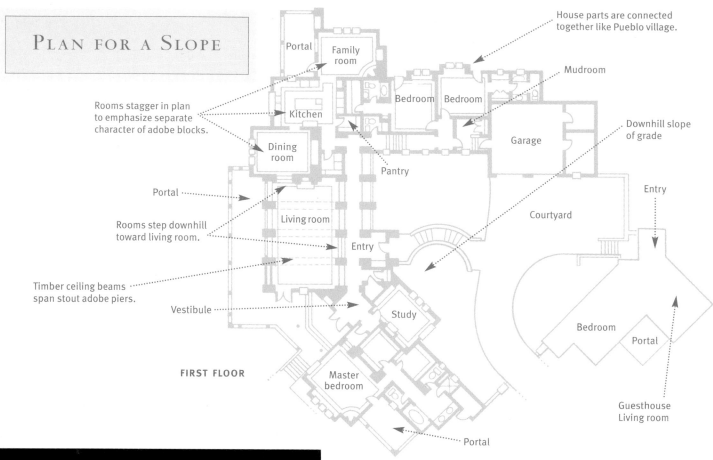

House parts are connected together like Pueblo village.

Mudroom

Downhill slope of grade

Portal

Family room

Bedroom   Bedroom

Garage

Entry

Rooms stagger in plan to emphasize separate character of adobe blocks.

Kitchen

Dining room

Pantry

Courtyard

Portal

Living room

Rooms step downhill toward living room.

Entry

Timber ceiling beams span stout adobe piers.

Vestibule

Study

Bedroom

Portal

FIRST FLOOR

Master bedroom

Guesthouse Living room

Portal

The front door is made of heavy hand-planed planks with wrought iron hardware. The floor is paved in 16-in.-sq. Mexican terra-cotta tiles set in a diamond pattern.

The heavy, square-cut ceiling beams are supported by carved brackets, called corbels, *with arrowhead detailing, a design borrowed from the architecture of the Spanish missions.*

A heavy timber ceiling spans the living room, with the finished roof laid on top of layers of wooden beams. The squared beams support a layer of round logs, called vigas. *Rows of wood saplings are laid on top in a herringbone pattern, called* latillas.

The result is an interior of intimate places, each room housed in a discrete architectural building block, where it acquires a unique visual signature and quiet seclusion.

The ambiance of the living room is hushed and infused with a soft light, much like that of the interior of an old Spanish mission church. The walls are shaped of stark white gypsum plaster. High above, wooden beams span between adobe piers to accentuate the lofty form of the room and to provide a rhythmic cadence to the long walls. On top of each pier, a figurative wooden bracket, or *corbel*, carries the end of a hand-hewn ceiling beam, which is decorated with incised carving.

The ceiling is an intricate lattice of hewn wooden beams with round log *vigas* laid across them that, in turn, support a herringbone pattern of wood saplings, called *latillas*. Common in Spanish mission churches of the seventeenth century, the layered latticework ceiling combines the *vigas* of ancient adobe buildings with the ornate carved beams of the Spanish tradition.

SPANISH FLOORS AND CEILINGS

From the living room, which is the lowest point of the house, the floor level changes in response to the sloped ground of the rambling hillside site. The dining room is a separate alcove of space connected to the living room by a short flight of stairs. Floors paved in large Mexican terra-cotta tiles are set in a diamond pattern and flow from room to room, providing consistency. The tiles recall the fired-clay tile

The ambiance of the interior is hushed and infused with a soft light, much like that of the inside of an old Spanish mission church.

The rounded fireplace in the master bedroom is a beehive kiva, *a traditional Pueblo Indian design. Logs were stacked vertically in the small elliptical fireplace.*

floors imported by the Spanish, which eventually replaced the hard-packed clay floors of traditional adobe homes.

The kitchen (shown on page 48) is located in its own adobe building block. It is offset from the dining room and situated on the same floor level, but there is no straight passage or alignment between the two rooms. The architect constructed these interconnected rooms in a staggered pattern to mimic the rambling, picturesque floor plans of Pueblo architecture. The traditional ceiling of the kitchen is made of barrel vaults that rest on top of round log *vigas*, a form of vaulted ceiling introduced by the Spanish, who understood the mechanics of building with arches.

LIVING ON THE PORTALE

Rooms in traditional Spanish-Pueblo adobe houses were often connected by open-air patios surrounded by covered walkways or porches, called *portales* (shown on page 57). This Spanish design concept has been incorporated into contemporary adobe architecture, and here the *portale* has become an outdoor room. In this new old home, the *portale* extends across the room wall to take in views of the distant city. It is a traditional porch fashioned from posts and beams that are set into the adobe walls of the house. The combination of adobe and Old World Spanish touches, like the *portale*, provides a rich blend of tradition and elegance in this historic-looking new old home.

The cross hall is a rhythmic series of stucco frames spanned by wooden lintel beams that emphasize the depth of the thick masonry walls. The walls are finished with white gypsum plaster, which is troweled smooth but softly rounded at the corners in imitation of the lime-plastered walls of ancient adobes. Seating benches, called bancos, *are built in under the windows between the thick frames.*

AN HONEST
PRAIRIE
FARMHOUSE

First-time homebuilders Steve and Anna Easudes fell in love with Greek Revival-style farmhouses after years of touring the countryside of southeastern Michigan. So it was synchronicity that led them to purchase 25 acres with a deed that allowed them to build only a Greek Revival–style home on the property. They were only too happy to oblige.

For their 1830s-period Greek Revival farmhouse, the Easudeses insisted on authentic interior details such as old-fashioned push-button light switches and cast-iron rimlocks.

But the Easudeses didn't want their farmhouse to look like a historic-period replica, locked in time. Instead, they liked the way rambling Michigan farmhouses from the mid-nineteenth century were enlarged in stages, with additions to meet the needs of growing families. The farmhouse is new, but it resembles an 1830s home that was enlarged in phases over a period of 100 years. Inside, unadorned spaces, salvaged period fixtures, and classic Greek Revival details make the new house look like a nineteenth-century relic.

SEARCHING FOR A MODEL

The Easudeses realized that to build an authentic new old house, it would be easier to recreate an old farmhouse by studying the details from a model. They searched the back-country roads for Greek

New England farmers who migrated to the Midwest in the 1830s and 1840s brought the popular Greek Revival style to the plains, simplifying the form to meet modest means.

Revival farmhouses but ultimately found the house that would inspire them in a museum.

The homeowners were drawn to the Plymouth House, a modest Greek Revival farmhouse they spotted at the Henry Ford Museum and Greenfield Village in Dearborn, Michigan. Its unassuming scale of two stories under a shallow roof with a smaller wing and front porch provided the ideal model of a welcoming family home that was authentic, but unpretentious. They asked the museum for measured drawings of the historic house and turned them over to architect Marc Rueter. Soon their new Greek Revival farmhouse began to take shape.

The new old house recreates the simplified details of Midwestern Greek Revival architecture developed long ago by rural craftsmen. Many of the moldings and decorative motifs that builders used in the 1830s were learned from pattern books but were simplified into forms that farmers could easily build.

The farmhouse that Marc designed closely follows the lines and layout of Plymouth House. The two-story house is a plain box in the shape of a small Greek temple, resembling a Monopoly piece, with its low-pitched roof and elementary form. In typical Greek Revival style, the gable end of the roof faces forward, and a wide frieze band of flat boards skirts beneath the roof.

ENLARGING THE PROPORTIONS

Marc worked on a scaled-up version of the historic house, enlarging the floor plan and overall dimensions to make the house slightly bigger. But he was careful to retain the original balanced relationship among the building parts. As the proportions of the facade grew in height and width, so too did the relative size of windows, doors, columns, and trim moldings. Each detail was enlarged in keeping with

Tall double-hung windows are divided into multiple panes by traditional wooden muntins. Window casings are simple square-edged boards shaped into a shallow pediment with a molded hood.

hallmarks of style
GREEK REVIVAL IN THE MIDWEST

The earliest southeastern Michigan farms date from the second quarter of the nineteenth century, when ambitious New Englanders and discontented New York farmers headed to the new Northwest Territory, bringing with them Greek Revival architecture.

By 1830, Greek Revival was known as "the national style," because it was the first truly American style of architecture. Houses that looked like miniature Greek temples sprouted across the frontier. Most of the farmhouses were modest country renditions of the classical style, with simplified designs to suit the means of farmers who nevertheless wanted to display their prosperity and good taste.

Such a farmhouse resembled a diminutive Parthenon, but without the encircling row of columns. Seldom do classical columns decorate the facades of farmhouses, as they often do in urban Greek Revival houses, as this purely decorative ornament was an expensive luxury for the average farmer. Most surviving period farmhouses are picturesque compositions of adaptations and additions of the style.

the new scale of the house to preserve its authenticity. For instance, Marc made the double-hung windows on the ground floor taller to accent the vertical dimension of the main house, thinking the Plymouth House was somewhat short and squat. In his adaptation, he also raised the low ceiling heights of the original model from 7 ft. to 8 ft. 6 in. on the first floor and 8 ft. on the second floor. The added ceiling height made it possible to introduce more light into the upstairs bedrooms through small attic windows. These windows are framed in the exterior frieze band that runs under the roof eaves.

Recognizing the importance of perfectly balanced symmetry in Greek Revival architecture, the architect placed three rows of evenly spaced windows on the long wall of the main house. To recreate the look of old-fashioned windows, the Easudeses chose to use wooden double-hung sashes with single glazing, instead of insulated glass, and real wooden muntins between the panes. They also installed traditional wooden storm windows and screen panels, but these need to be changed twice yearly between seasons, adding a commitment of labor to one of historical accuracy.

A RAMBLING FLOOR PLAN

The compact temple form of early Greek Revival houses seldom provided for all the spatial needs of the typical farm family. The simple temple soon became the center of a rambling warren of rooms, as wings to accommodate kitchens, pantries, work rooms, and even additional bedrooms were added to the primary structure. Most of the historic Greek

ARCHITECTURAL DETAILS
CLASSICAL ORDER

Greek Revival style is considered classical because it uses simplified architectural details from the classical orders, a decorative system of columns, beams, and pediments that the ancient Greeks used for their temples.

A Greek Revival farmhouse often mimics the temple in shape alone: a rectangular box of plain walls covered by a shallow roof with its gable facing forward. The columns almost disappear, replaced by pilasters, or wide corner boards with a molded cap, that stand in for columns. These pilasters support a deep frieze band that imitates a classical entablature, or heavy roof beam.

In a classical order, a triangular pediment sits on top of the columns and entablature. The Greek Revival style reduces the pediment to a molded roof cornice with short cornice returns, to suggest the complete triangle of a pediment. The simplified details of the Greek Revival are meant to look like a diminutive temple.

For classical symmetry, the architect placed three tall windows perfectly spaced along the side walls of the ground floor. Small second-floor attic windows are found high up beneath the cornice. They bring light and air inside but are set too high to provide a view.

As the proportions of the facade grew in height and width, so too did the relative size of windows, doors, columns, and trim moldings.

A GREEK TEMPLE

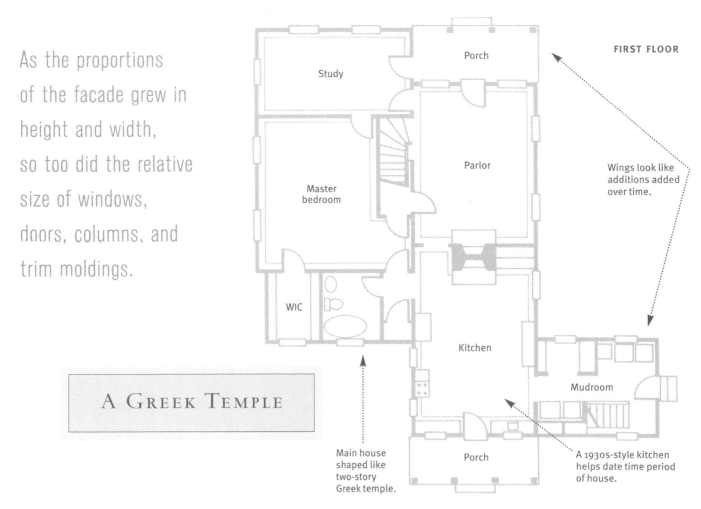

FIRST FLOOR

Porch

Study

Parlor

Master bedroom

WIC

Kitchen

Mudroom

Wings look like additions added over time.

Main house shaped like two-story Greek temple.

Porch

A 1930s-style kitchen helps date time period of house.

Inside, unadorned spaces, salvaged period fixtures, and classic Greek Revival details make the new house look like a nineteenth-century relic.

The mantelpiece and fitted cupboards in the living room were reproduced from historic houses at Greenfield Village. To keep the house looking untouched by modern mechanical systems, the homeowners avoided holes for ductwork by installing radiant heating coils in the floor structure.

Revival farmhouses we see today are the result of layers of additions over many years.

In their new old house, the Easudeses wanted to capture the appearance of a house that grew over time with a string of additions. So the layout of the floor plan incorporates make-believe additions from several time periods: first, a front porch and new parlor, followed by a kitchen, then a pantry and mudroom, and finally a back porch. These single-story sections collect around the "original" portion of the house, now occupied by the master bedroom and a small study. The unconventional floor plan redistributes rooms in unexpected locations, placing the living room and kitchen in a side wing attached to the two-story temple form.

This room arrangement mimics the way a real farmhouse would have evolved. Each wing, from the parlor to the kitchen to the mudroom, simulates the ad hoc way in which additions were historically integrated into the farmhouse plan, giving the house the rambling appearance the Easudeses wanted.

PLAIN FARMHOUSE INTERIORS

The details of the interior are farmhouse plain— simple and unornamented like the practical finishes that old-time farmers would have used. The baseboard and casing trim for the windows and doors are square boards without molded edges. And to make the house truly authentic, the homeowners insisted that the builder install the casing trims first and then fit the gypsum wallboard around them, imitating the old method of plastering walls after the trim moldings were applied.

Amid these austere interior finishes, the hardware fittings are eye-catching details. Old-style push-button switches and brass switch plates for the electrical fixtures add small moments of history. On each of the raised-panel doors, the clay pottery

The mudroom wing looks like a miniature temple. The molding above the door trim is called a hood.

knobs and cast-iron rimlocks are salvaged antique fittings common in the late nineteenth century. These old-fashioned fittings are tiny timepieces that add hints of age throughout the house.

BUILDING AROUND A STOVE

The Easudeses planned the story of their house to seem as if nothing had been changed since the 1930s. They wanted the house to have accumulated alterations up to the Depression and to have never been touched again. Sealed in the past, like garden preserves, the farmhouse *Tells a Story Over Time* that is enriched with period furnishings.

The kitchen is designed with a Depression-era flavor, captured in a restored porcelain gas range. On either side of the range are a sideboard and a classic Hoosier cabinet, a period piece that completes the 1920s aura of the space. These details act as the finale in the story of this new old nineteenth-century-style home.

TRADITIONAL CRAFTSMANSHIP
SALVAGED HARDWARE

→ One way to enhance the old-fashioned character of a new house is to install antique hardware on doors, walls, and cabinets. Period hardware fixtures accent the historical authenticity of the house by drawing attention to the working parts of the interiors. Doorknobs and switches are tactile details used daily by all who live in and visit the house, reminding them of the history behind the design.

The homeowners searched for and found old clay pottery knobs, in marbleized and jet-black patterns, and iron rimlocks that were classic

hardware sets commonly used in the nineteenth century. The cast-iron rimlocks are durably constructed with simple mechanisms that can be easily restored and kept in good working order.

Antique locksets can be found in most architectural salvage stores and reproductions can be bought through specialty hardware suppliers.

The homeowners wanted a Depression-era kitchen to make the house look as if it were finished in the 1930s. The kitchen is furnished with freestanding appliances rather than fitted cabinetry. The 1928 porcelain Glazier stove and Hoosier cabinet bring authenticity to the room.

RELOCATING
A RELIC

Looking for the perfect old house can lead you on a journey far and wide. But what do you do when you find a real treasure in a place far from home? For Alan and Ilona Croft, the answer was simple—you move it. They now live in a transplanted historic house that they boxed up and moved from Connecticut to Virginia, carefully restored as a family home rather than as a museum.

Nine Brothers Farm, built in 1790, was moved piece by piece from Connecticut and reconstructed in Virginia. The wall paneling in this new old room, in random widths up to 24 in. wide, is made of the attic floorboards salvaged from the original house.

The eighteenth-century farmhouse shows the details of Georgian architecture: fluted pilaster columns and a front door framed by a portico with a pedimented roof.

The Crofts found their piece of moveable history in Preston, Connecticut. The tattered Connecticut Valley Colonial-style farmhouse, called Nine Brothers Farm, was about to be torn down. They faced daunting challenges in turning a rundown historic jewel into a working home, a process that required dismantling the house, moving it piece by piece, and rebuilding it in Virginia.

In their pursuit of authenticity, the Crofts made painful decisions about which original materials to save and which to throw out before making the trip back to Virginia. Some parts of the dilapidated house were too far gone to salvage, whereas others, such as the heavy stone foundation, were too expensive to transport. Once the pieces were moved to Virginia, the homeowners had to find an appropriate setting,

where the rebuilt house would look at home, showing *Respect for the Character of Place*. But the new house could not simply be a restored relic. In converting the old farmhouse into a working home, the Crofts needed to rethink the historic floor plan to meet the needs of modern family living.

A FARAWAY FIND

Built in 1790 by Nathan Ayer, Nine Brothers Farm is an authentic example of the Connecticut Valley Colonial style, with traditional details, such as the symmetrical facade of five window bays, classical front doorway, and carved corner pilaster columns. But the years had taken their toll on the house: the facades had been stripped of their historic details, and the walls had been covered with asbestos siding.

New beveled pine clapboards are fastened with eighteenth-century wrought-iron rose-head nails salvaged from the original house. The nails were still usable, even after 200 years of weathering.

Underneath the house's derelict appearance, the Crofts could see the outlines of a real gem, and their instincts were confirmed by a visit to the Preston Historical Society. An old photograph of the farm from the 1930s showed the original facade with all of its classical trimmings intact. Their disheveled discovery was actually a true classic awaiting restoration.

Back in Virginia, the Crofts purchased a vacant farmstead that was suited to a colonial farmhouse. They searched their new acreage for an established setting, a place where the house would be able to complement the land, but not be perched on the highest point of ground. Like the early colonial builders, they wanted a site that was protected from the weather, sheltered by trees, and had a natural saddle or rise on which to set the house. The homeowners found a perfect spot on a knoll where the land rose near a bend in the creek.

hallmarks of style
CONNECTICUT VALLEY COLONIAL

The Georgian (1720–1790) houses of the Connecticut River Valley were constructed with classical details and decorative facades of ornamental woodwork. A classical door surround composed of columns and a pediment was the signature feature of the style, often enhanced with a transom or fanlight window above the door. Exterior walls were finished with tightly spaced painted clapboards trimmed by corner pilaster columns and an elaborate molded cornice, just as at Nine Brothers Farm.

In the Connecticut River Valley, the early colonial hall-and-parlor plan was common. A massive chimney in the middle of the house was flanked by a front hall and a parlor with a keeping room across the back.

The entrance vestibule and a compact winder stair were packed into the space between the front door and chimney. The keeping room is where most of the family chores were done. Smaller rooms were divided off at each end for a larder and a borning room to nurse infants.

Typical of a Connecticut Valley Colonial, the compact entry vestibule doubles as a compact stair hall. The tight winder stair is pinched into the wall.

The woodwork, including the mantelpiece, crown molding, and chair rail, was restored in its original location. Shutters, which help retain heat in winter, slide on grooves cut into the molding.

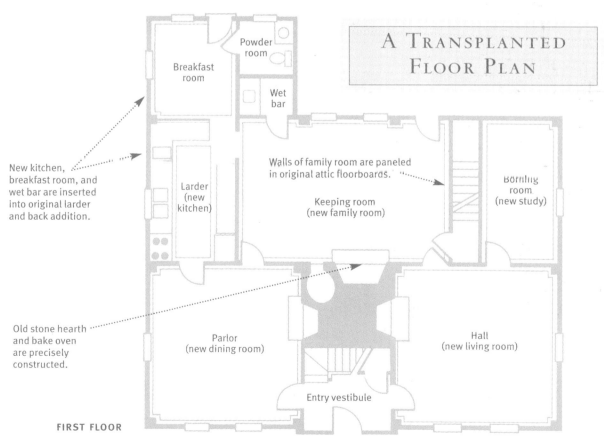

A TRANSPLANTED FLOOR PLAN

Powder room

Breakfast room

Wet bar

New kitchen, breakfast room, and wet bar are inserted into original larder and back addition.

Larder (new kitchen)

Walls of family room are paneled in original attic floorboards.

Keeping room (new family room)

Borning room (new study)

Old stone hearth and bake oven are precisely constructed.

Parlor (new dining room)

Hall (new living room)

Entry vestibule

FIRST FLOOR

TO SAVE OR NOT TO SAVE

The Crofts realized they would have to take apart the old farmhouse to move it across five states. But how much of the original structure could they realistically transport? The rough stone foundations and hidden chimney bricks would be expensive to move, so they decided not to bring them back to Virginia. But they realized the historic value of the mortise-and-tenon wood frame, the exterior moldings, the stone fireplaces, the wide oak floorboards, the paneled interior walls, and even all of the old hand-forged nails (shown on page 73). These salvaged elements are *Details for Authenticity* that are important for recording the history of the house and essential to telling its story.

A new wet bar, designed to resemble a miniature colonial pub, fits into a corner of the keeping room. Wooden door grilles and beaded wall boards recall details of historic woodwork.

Reinstalled throughout the house, the salvaged artifacts are authentic bits of history that preserve the true antique patina of age.

The Crofts hired the same carpenters who dismantled the Connecticut house to reconstruct it in Virginia. When rebuilding, the craftsmen used old photographs of the farmhouse to recreate missing historic details. For example, they reproduced the square fluted columns and pedestal bases of the corner pilasters as well as the intricate cornice moldings, including the dentils, which resemble a row of wooden teeth (shown on page 80).

Typical of many old houses, parts of the timber sills and beams that made up the first-floor frame were rotted away. To replace them, the carpenters fashioned new hand-hewn oak sills and floor beams in the original sizes and set them in place. The rest of the timber frame structure was simply pegged back together again, illustrating the beauty of posts and beams fastened by mortise-and-tenon joints, which fit together like a kit of parts.

The siding on the old farmhouse posed a similar problem. In a shortsighted 1940s remodeling, the original clapboard siding had been covered with asbestos shingles, causing the wood to rot from moisture trapped underneath. The rebuilt house was sided with new clapboards from New England, cut to the same profile as the original boards. The homeowners collected all of the hand-forged rosehead nails from the old farmhouse, which were still strong even after 200 years of weathering, to fasten the new clapboard siding in place.

KEEPING INTERIORS INTACT

The original interior was in no better shape than the exterior. Typical of late-eighteenth-century construction, the old walls were finished with horsehair plaster (lime plaster with horsehair as binder) applied over strips of wooden lath. But the plaster walls were badly cracked and patched in many places and could not be saved. Instead, the Crofts re-plastered the interior walls, but kept pieces of the old wooden lath to build a replica wall, showing the plaster-on-lath technique. The exhibit panel is on display inside the stairwell to the basement.

Some pieces of history were too significant to throw away. The Crofts realized that the old oak

The massive stone fireplace in the keeping room was the original cooking hearth, with a bake oven inset into the stonework. Each stone was numbered and graphed before the hearth was dismantled, so the fireplace could be accurately reconstructed. An antique wrought-iron pot crane hangs inside on iron pintle hinges.

The plank exterior door into the back addition is mounted on salvaged wrought-iron strap hinges with decorative split bracket ends. Strap hinges were used in the 1700s to support heavy doors.

The Crofts realized the historic value of the mortise-and-tenon wood frame, the exterior moldings, the stone fireplaces, and the wide oak floorboards.

floorboards, up to 2 ft. wide, were treasures. The Crofts saved them all and cataloged their locations so the boards could be placed exactly in the new house using the hand-forged nails. Even the attic floorboards were saved to be refashioned as beaded paneling. Along with the many raised-panel interior doors, the Crofts saved all of the wrought-iron H-L hinges, strap hinges, cast-iron thumb latches, boxlocks, and other pieces of period hardware that had historic value. Reinstalled throughout the house, these salvaged artifacts are authentic bits of the past that preserve the true antique patina of age.

ADJUSTING AN OUTDATED FLOOR PLAN

Making decisions about what stays and what goes helped the Crofts consider changing the floor plan as they rebuilt the house. The layouts of most old houses don't accommodate the needs of modern family living, and the house from Connecticut was no exception. The old house did not have a modern kitchen or any bathrooms, other than an outhouse. Even clothes closets were missing, because in the eighteenth century, clothing and linens were stored in wardrobes and chests.

The classic New England colonial floor plan of Nine Brothers Farm—called a hall-and-parlor plan—had two identical rooms for the hall and parlor in the front of the house and a keeping room/kitchen across the back, with smaller rooms at the back corners. The homeowners reorganized the traditional plan by making discrete alterations that would accommodate their daily functions and yet keep the authenticity of the house intact. Many of their needs could be knit into the existing pattern of rooms by preserving the formal rooms under new names and by partitioning and refitting the secondary spaces for new uses.

The twin parlors were reconstructed exactly as they were in the old house, but renamed as the liv-

The original farmhouse had a lean-to addition on the back, called a buttery, which was slightly enlarged in the reconstruction. The neatly squared stones used for the foundation are some of the original pieces saved from the old structure.

Top left: At the top of the corner pilasters, a square version of a classical capital crowns the pilaster. The cornice, copied from old photographs, is detailed with a continuous notched molding, called a dentil, that looks like a row of wooden teeth.

Bottom left: The pilasters, or flat columns set into the wall of the house, are elaborate, decorative corner boards that appear to support the weight of the roof. The column shaft is fluted with a series of vertical channels, and sits on top of a pedestal base.

ing room and dining room. The craftsmen restored the original mantelpieces, crown moldings, and chair rails in these rooms, and accurately reconstructed the cut-stone hearths. They also found the missing raised-panel interior shutters—which had been neatly cut in half to make cabinet doors—spliced them together again, and set them in their old locations.

The original keeping room—the old-fashioned equivalent of an all-purpose room where colonial families cooked, worked, and gathered together—was the perfect size for the Crofts' new family room (shown on page 77). The room centers on an enormous stone cooking fireplace with a bake oven embedded in one side, authentically rebuilt to add to the historic character of this updated farmhouse.

TRADITIONAL CRAFTSMANSHIP
FIELDSTONE WALLS

Dry-stacked stone walls are typical of both the rural New England countryside and the foothills of the Blue Ridge Mountains in Virginia. As farmers plowed and cleared their land, they would pile stones at the edges of the fields to mark off boundaries. The traditional Virginia fieldstone wall is made of rough stones laid up without mortar. The sides of the wall are battered, or leaned in at a slight angle, and flat stones are placed across the top to form a cap. Although they appear crudely constructed, fieldstone walls can stand for a century with only minor repairs. Together with four-board fences, the fieldstone walls are still a hallmark of the rural Virginia landscape.

A NEW
FARMSTEAD
WITH A
PAST

Antique farmhouses are patchwork structures with layers of renovations and additions, each one telling a tale about how the place grew from generation to generation. Houses became enlarged to accommodate growing families, each addition recording a chapter in the history of American farm life.

In this new old Pennsylvania Dutch farmhouse, the floors are old oak barn boards of random widths that were lightly sanded to reveal mottled shades of caramel to black. Floors were then finished with tung oil and butcher's wax.

This farmhouse, built in Pennsylvania, is a new home created to look like a sturdy, rambling farmstead that changed its shape over time to incorporate shifting family needs. Built in sections of log, stone, and clapboard, the house shares the traditions of the eighteenth-century farmhouses that populate the surrounding Brandywine Valley.

The new farmhouse sits on a fold in the land halfway down the hill, situated much like the Pennsylvania Dutch farmers would have done. Rather than building their houses on the highest ground, the early settlers placed them facing south and banked them into a hillside. A mid-slope setting was a practical decision, chosen to take advantage of the warmth of the southern sun and the protection from the north winds offered by the crest of a hill.

Architect Peter Zimmerman studied the ways the old local houses evolved and added these architectural forms in layers to convey the look and feel of a house rich with history. The house is made of logs and fieldstone, *Crafted with Natural Materials*, and assembled in ways the old and frugal German builders and craftsmen would have used. Markings of recent renovations were built into the additions to create the perception that the home is still being remodeled, even after all these years, showing how a new old house can *Incorporate Modern Conveniences*.

The layered-on and aged additions are clearly seen from fields at the back of the house. The house looks as if it had rambling collections of additions that accumulated over many generations. The architect recreated a house with distinct building periods, from an early log cabin that extended into a stone house, followed by a clapboard addition and a carriage barn. Formed in a cluster, one part is attached to the next in a growing chain of additions.

A RAMBLING TALE

The new old farmhouse looks cobbled together from many parts—a rambling stone house pieced together with generations of additions. One end of the stone house is joined to a log cabin and the other is attached to a smaller stone wing and a wood clapboard addition. Peter created the new house around the history of authentic Pennsylvania Dutch farmsteads.

The tale of the farmstead begins with a family of German settlers who built a log house on their eighteenth-century land grant. Although the story is make believe, it appears that a fire destroyed one end of the log house, and the farmers decided to rebuild

PENNSYLVANIA DUTCH FARMSTEAD

erman immigrants to Pennsylvania in the late seventeenth century, known today as the Pennsylvania Dutch, turned the fertile crescent of land west of Philadelphia into productive farmsteads They first built houses of logs on their newly cleared croplands. Later, they erected permanent houses using stones gathered from the fields and traditional building skills they brought from their homeland.

Massive stone walls were built 2 ft. thick by laying together sturdy fieldstones. Peeled oak logs were used for floor beams and roof rafters, with rough-sawn planks for floors and partition walls. The roofs were covered with split-oak shingles. The interior stone walls were finished with lime plaster and were kept looking clean with periodic coats of whitewash.

As generations passed, the frugal German settlers expanded their farmhouses by adding on new wings rather than by rebuilding, creating the picturesque structures made of log and stone additions that we see today.

by adding a larger stone house onto the burned end. Still later, the fictional history goes, a stone wing was added with a new front entrance door and porch. Then a clapboard wing and a carriage barn were built to complete the fictional changes.

The carriage barn garage is attached to the log house by a covered walkway. Built of stone and clapboard, the building has a turn-of-the-last-century character, because its distinctive out-swinging doors seem originally designed for carriages rather than cars. The garage doesn't overpower the house, since the third bay is designed as a clapboard addition attached to the side of the original stone section.

This clever ruse makes the three-car garage look smaller, diminishing its scale in relation to the house.

MAKING A LOG HOUSE

A crescent-shaped covered walk connects the carriage barn to the log wing of the house. Built of salvaged antique timbers, the log wing is the original dwelling in the make-believe story of the farm, although it now looks like a minor addition in the overall plan. Many early German farmsteads in the Brandywine Valley started out as log cabins just like this one. Its walls are V-notched together at the cor-

---

ARCHITECTURAL DETAILS
EVOLUTION OF THE BREEZEWAY

→ The historic model for a breezeway comes from England, where medieval English churchyards had covered walkways between buildings. These covered walkways were made of hewn timber posts that supported a roof structure of beams and rafters framed together in triangles, called trusses. For the new breezeway on this home, the architect used English timber-frame details for the roof trusses.

Although the breezeway that connects the carriage barn to the log house is not a historic feature for a German farmhouse, the version on this house is designed to look like one. The architect *Invented within the Rules* of style to

The open breezeway connects the house to the garage. The heavy timber beams form a series of triangle frames.

interpret the traditions and materials of the Pennsylvania Dutch style in a new building part. The breezeway seems to fit because it borrows details for its fieldstone base, timber posts, and shingled roof from the architecture of the house.

At the front of the house, a gravel parking circle is carved out of the slope of the hill and edged with a fieldstone retaining wall. The wings of the house and carriage barn fold around the circle to create a sheltering enclosure; the breezeway helps link the front and back views.

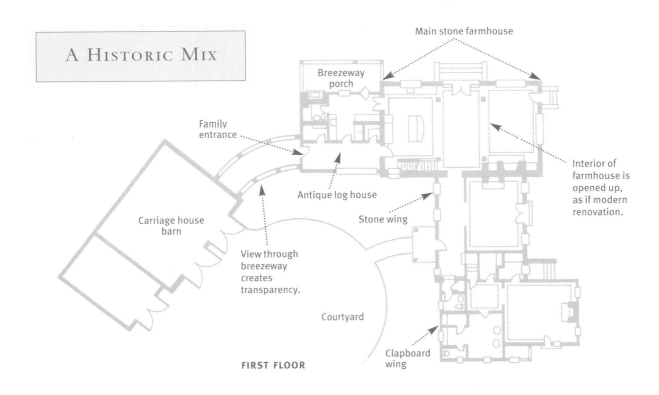

A HISTORIC MIX

Main stone farmhouse

Breezeway porch

Family entrance

Antique log house

Carriage house barn

View through breezeway creates transparency.

Stone wing

Interior of farmhouse is opened up, as if modern renovation.

Courtyard

Clapboard wing

FIRST FLOOR

The old log timbers of the cabin are hewn with squared faces, and the spaces between the logs are filled in with white chinking mortar. While the cabin is not a reconstructed old building, rough-sawn ceiling joists stained dark and wide antique oak floorboards make it appear to be vintage.

The billiard-room mantel wall is plastered and painted so that every surface is clean and white. Early fieldstone fireboxes, like the one recreated here, were often plastered on the inside to prevent the fire from burning the limestone and mortar joints.

ners, like Lincoln Logs, and the spaces between are filled with a traditional chinking covered with mortar.

The family entrance door is under the curved breezeway of the log house. Inside the doorway, the rough-hewn log walls are exposed in the entry hall, and antique oak floors strengthen the illusion that this section is truly old. Electrified wall sconces are modified reproductions of colonial-era candle sticks. The log section also has remnants of a pretend old kitchen, which is now used as a pantry, fitted with colonial-style cabinets (to hide appliances) and an old-fashioned ceramic farm sink—pieces of the fictional saga behind this new old house.

THE LOOK OF OLD STONE

The stone house is built of a mixture of limestone and sandstone harvested in the Schuylkill River Valley. Called Chesterfield Blend, the stone mix looks like the tan and iron brown fieldstone that the Pennsylvania Dutch farmers used to build farmhouse walls. As in the German masonry tradition, the irregular stones are fitted together in random courses, like a wall puzzle made of odd shapes, and the joints are filled with a light brown sand mortar.

This traditional stonework is featured on the small stone wing addition, where the formal paneled

The thoughtful layout of the new house is really a fictional story of renovations made to an old farmhouse.

The first floor of the stone house is opened as one large great room for the living room, dining room, and kitchen. The rough-sawn ceiling timbers have split, or checked, as they dried out, leaving cracks in the faces that look old when saturated with tung oil.

*A massive stone fireplace, 12 ft. across with a mantel-tree beam, brings the field-
stone inside, anchoring the living room section of the great room. The hearth is made of
antique bricks.*

AGING A STONE WALL TODAY

Among building materials for walls, stone remains one of the most durable, yet expensive, options. A house made of true stone walls is *Built for the Ages,* like the 8-in.-thick stone veneer on this house. But stones must be laid by skilled masons who can fit odd-shaped fieldstones into a pleasing pattern. This handwork takes patience, progress is slow, and it inevitably costs more than simple framing.

The Chesterfield Blend stonework used on the farmhouse is a mixture of Schuylkill River Valley limestone and sandstone blended to simulate classic Pennsylvania fieldstone. A special mortar mixture is used for setting the stones that looks like the weathered lime mortar seen on many old farmhouses, made from white Portland cement and coarse brown construction sand.

The joints between the stones are tuck pointed, or filled with mortar, to make them weathertight and flush with the stone face. To *Create the Patina of Age,* the stones were drenched with a cocktail of aging ingredients called a slurry.

A SLURRY RECIPE The slurry used is a homegrown concoction that hastens the aging of stone walls in a matter of months, rather than decades. The slurry is a soupy mixture made of buttermilk, mold spores, beer, and a bit of cow manure. The broth is then brushed onto the stonework and left to react with the environment. The ingredients spoil on the walls, turning them tan brown and promoting mildew growth to cultivate a time-weathered look.

On the back wall, where the full shape of the main stone house is visible, the facade is designed with new windows and French doors to look as if it were recently remodeled.

The details of this entrance convey an updated historic makeover, including granite curbstones for the door threshold, antique brick stair platforms, and a pent roof of hand-split shingles with timber brackets.

front door with its transom window fits underneath a covered porch on square wood posts (shown on page 83). The stone and carpentry work are a perfect match for historic colonial details, replicating the window frames and paneled wood shutters that graced early Pennsylvania Dutch farmhouses. As in the story of the house, the architect has taken care to *Detail for Authenticity*.

The back facade of the house is designed to look as if it had been recently remodeled. Groups of new windows and French doors, which capture views of the pastoral landscape, have altered the old-looking stone facade, leaving the telltale marks of an imaginary renovation. Such touches of updating, both inside and out, *Incorporate Modern Conveniences* into this new old farmhouse.

The timber-framed porch, covered by a roof built of hand-split wood shingles, frames views of the bucolic countryside of the Brandywine Valley.

BUILDING
BY THE
BOOK

When you have your heart set on an old house and then decide to build new, there is a special incentive to make the new house look authentic. Getting there means becoming an architectural sleuth who tracks down examples of old houses to learn from. Architect Gil Schafer used his professional observations and research tools to help him create a new vintage house.

The entry hall floors are 200-year-old heart pine finished with tung oil and then carnauba wax to preserve their original surface patina. The unusual panel-within-panel design for the new front door is inspired by measured drawings of regional Greek Revival doorways.

Drawing on the Greek Revival style of classical farmhouses in Upstate New York, the new design re-creates the proportions and details of houses from 1820 to 1850. A monumental row of Greek Doric columns supports the front portico.

Gil had already spent years looking for an old farmhouse to restore in the Hudson Valley when he finally decided to buy vacant farmland and start from scratch. Then he hunted for old houses and surveys of historic details for the regional Greek Revival style of 1820–1850 that he admired. This footwork helped him design an authentic new old house and cultivate convincing period interiors by incorporating antique materials and reproduction fittings. By adding *Details for Authenticity* and *Creating the Patina of Age,* Gil recreated a Greek Revival home for himself that looks like it has a long history.

The architect built his new version of a classic Greek Revival house of the 1830s on a piece of idyllic, rural country property. He chose a house site on a green saddle of land between two hillsides. Stone walls and hedged gardens form a frame of landscaping around the house, features that attach the house to the land and extend the reach of the architecture into the fields. The new house *Respects the Character of Place*, complementing the lay of the land so that the setting looks established.

USING PATTERN BOOKS

The architectural details of the house are so convincing that is hard to believe the house is new. From the pristine white exterior to the proportions of the columns and profiles of the moldings, every aspect falls into place with the precision of an old house. To achieve this, Gil studied the same early-

From the pristine exterior to the proportions of the columns, every aspect falls into place with the precision of an old house.

nineteenth-century pattern books that guided the original Greek Revival craftsmen in building houses.

Gil also used Carl Schmidt's modern study, *Greek Revival Details*, as a source for design ideas. He adapted the arrangement of the front doorway with its sidelights and transom window from measured drawings in the book. He also selected other period details that were suitable for his design and integrated them as elements, using the measured details he found in the text to authenticate his new house.

SIMULATED HISTORY

The house sits like a classical temple on its own acropolis. Upon closer study, the house has three distinct parts that look as if they had evolved over time. The main part of the house is shaped like a two-story Greek temple, with a majestic portico of columns across the front. Attached to one side is a story-and-a-half kitchen wing, with a small covered porch and attic windows. Running along the other side is a long, one-story screen porch. The temple front is monumental in scale, befitting its importance as the formal center of the house, while the modest kitchen wing is of simpler details that suit its secondary role, and the screen porch is a minor addition for an outdoor sitting room.

Each part simulates the changes that mark the history of an early-nineteenth-century Hudson Valley farmhouse. In this architectural fiction, the simple

hallmarks of style
GREEK REVIVAL STYLE

he Greek Revival style that flourished from 1820 to 1850 was born with the founding of the new American republic and was called the "national" style. The style derives its forms from the classical Greek temple, such as the Parthenon, where columns and beams support a shallow-pitched roof. Like a classical temple, the gable roof faces forward, creating a pediment, or triangle, which is supported on an entablature, or decorated beam, carried on top of columns.

The temple form of a Greek Revival house is often designed as a front portico that features a row of monumental columns, as in this new house.

Early-nineteenth-century Greek Revival houses were made of wood and sided with clapboards that were usually painted white. White had symbolic importance because it expressed the classical virtues of nobility and purity aspired to by the citizens of the young American republic.

kitchen wing might have been built first, followed by the elaborate main house and front portico, when prosperity allowed for a stylish addition. The scale and complexity of the details distinguish one building period from another: The details of one part are plain and of the other, fancy.

PROPORTIONED FACADES

This new old house's Greek Revival architecture is derived from the classical traditions of ancient Greece. The builders of antiquity used columns and horizontal beams as both the structure and the decorative scheme for buildings that were designed using strict rules of proportion. Columns support a

deep beam, called an entablature, that in turn carries the triangular pediment of the roof. The size of the columns governs the scale of the other details and decorative moldings.

Columns of different sizes distinguish the main house from the kitchen wing. Four robust Greek Doric columns support the two-story front portico, whereas three slender columns carry the covered porch of the wing. Though the sculptural details of the columns are the same, the smaller columns are half the size of the larger ones and the details are diminished proportionally. These changes of scale and proportion are the way classical architecture sets up a hierarchy of building parts.

ARCHITECTURAL DETAILS
OLD PATTERN BOOKS

→ Throughout history, American builders have used pattern books to learn the building elements, rules of proportion, and finished details for popular architectural styles. Most builders of the 1830s depended heavily on published pattern books of Greek Revival details for instruction. American architects Asher Benjamin in *The Architect, or Practical House Carpenter* (1830) and Minard Lafever in *The Beauties of Modern Architecture* (1835) published handbooks found everywhere in nineteenth-century builders' toolboxes. Gil used these pattern books as guides to build his new old house.

For details of the Greek Revival in Upstate New York, Gil turned to the surveys of local examples published in the 1960s by architectural historian Carl Schmidt. In his *Greek Revival*

Details of 1968, Schmidt includes meticulous measured drawings of columns, entablatures, doors and windows, mantelpieces, and molding profiles. Gil used this book as one of his guides, modeling the front entrance on a plate in the book.

A PLAIN BARN

Sitting beside the house is a simple barn turned garage. The barn's plain carpentry details of flat window casings and exposed roof rafters contrast with the elaborate main house. The board-and-batten garage is a respite from classical formality. Walls of vertical boards and the standing-seam metal roof are common details of barn architecture. Designed in the style of a small nineteenth-century carriage house, the garage is plain and simple, in the tradition of outbuildings on a Hudson Valley farm.

Simplified detailing continues on the back of the main house. The garden facade has no columns but retains the temple shape and triangular pediment of the front. Framed within walls of white clapboards, the three windows are evenly spaced across the facade in the perfect symmetry that is a hallmark of the Greek Revival style.

A graceful pergola, laced with climbing wisteria, provides a covered arbor over the back door. The pergola is an open grille of crossed timbers mounted on top of two columns, a form often used in turn-of-the-last-century garden architecture. Adapted to this Greek Revival house of the 1830s, the pergola illustrates how to *Invent within the Rules* of style.

AUTHENTIC HUDSON VALLEY INTERIORS

The homeowner not only wanted his new old house to look authentic but wanted the interior to create a portrait of the past fashioned for modern living, with finishes and fixtures that *Tell a Story Over Time* of a Hudson Valley farmhouse. Each detail adds color to the finished picture—floors that are centuries old, moldings that are pure Greek Revival, mantels that are nineteenth-century classics, and replica hardware that has a hand-rubbed patina.

Sided with vertical boards and batten strips, the barn/garage is detailed with exposed roof rafter tails and windows framed in flat casings, beneath a galvanized metal roof of standing seams.

Inside the front entry hall, the ornamental moldings have a commanding presence that is the hallmark of Greek Revival trimwork. Broad in width and cut in strong profiles, the door frames and crown moldings are striking to our modern eyes, which are accustomed to seeing spindly builders' trims. The crown molding at the ceiling rises in a deep undercut cove called a bird's beak, and the door casings are wide, flat boards edged with a carved backband that projects at the top corners to form dog's ears.

The house's age-mellowed wood floors have a 200-year-old story to tell. Bare-wood floors in the

Seen through French doors from the screen porch, the living room is informally furnished around a nineteenth-century mantelpiece. As an alternative to costly antique heart pine, the floors are carpeted with less formal woven sea grass. The doorway is trimmed in a typical Greek Revival casing with dog-eared corners.

front entry and stair hall are true antique boards reclaimed from an old house, with all the marks of age still showing. The floorboards preserve the scarred and warped surface patina that shows their age, but the backsides have been planed smooth so that they lay flat on the floor frame. They are finished with tung oil and carnauba wax for a dull luster that avoids the sheen of polyurethane.

Hand-finished hardware adds period touches. All of the doorknobs, hinges, switch plates, drawer pulls, and light fixtures in the house are new, but they have a well-used patina. Each piece of hardware is refinished with an antiquing process that recreates the mottled effects of age.

A SENSE OF SPACIOUSNESS

The home's floor plan has an off-center stair hall that runs down one side of the house from the front entry vestibule to the back door. This arrangement opens most of the first floor for double parlors, one for the living room and the other for a dining room/library. The parlors are separated by back-to-back fireplaces set in a thick partition wall, with doorways on either side to connect the two rooms in a free flow. The fireplaces are centered between the parlors, where a wide passageway would have been located in a historic Greek Revival floor plan. This new plan arrangement offers more separation and definition to both rooms.

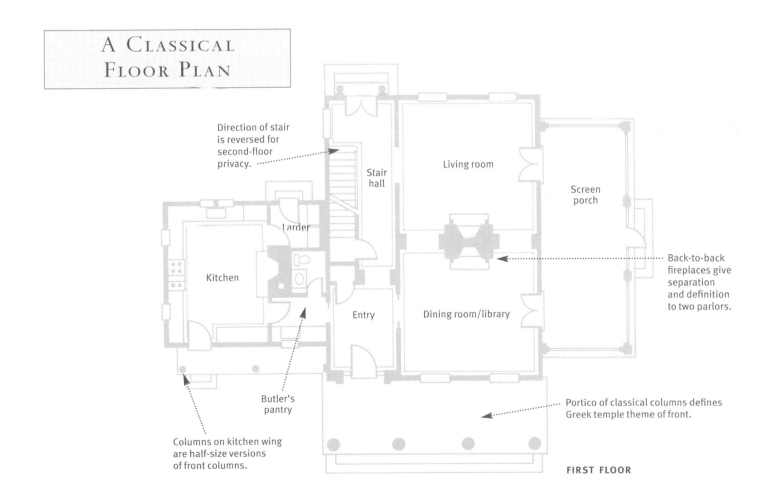

A CLASSICAL FLOOR PLAN

Direction of stair is reversed for second-floor privacy.

Stair hall

Living room

Screen porch

Larder

Kitchen

Back-to-back fireplaces give separation and definition to two parlors.

Entry

Dining room/library

Butler's pantry

Portico of classical columns defines Greek temple theme of front.

Columns on kitchen wing are half-size versions of front columns.

FIRST FLOOR

SILVERED GLASS DOORKNOBS

→ The silvered mercury glass doorknobs throughout the house were custom made from a mid-nineteenth-century pattern. The blown glass spheres are silvered on the inside for a brilliant appearance, which simulates the look of a precious metal. Each silvered knob is mounted on cast-brass backing plates, or shanks, that have an antique distressed patina.

Glass doorknobs were considered the epitome of elegance when they were first introduced in the 1800s, signifying purity and cleanliness. English glassmakers discovered a way to make silvered glassware using mercury in 1849, and then Enoch Robinson patented mercury glass in America in 1855. Today, Robinson's methods have been rediscovered. The silvered knobs of the 1850s are slightly later than the Greek Revival era, but the hardware has a period aura that reinforces the refinement of the house.

A long screen porch runs along the outside of the double parlors, with walls of beveled clapboard siding left exposed, as if the porch were screened in at a later date. The screen panels can be exchanged for glass panels in the winter to use the room in four seasons, a modern innovation that adapts the classic porch for contemporary living.

The new kitchen is detailed in turn-of-the-last-century style using glass-front wall cabinets and bin-pull drawer handles. The homespun interior is detailed with a hearth, beadboard paneling, and wide plank floors.

Few interior doors interrupt the flow of the floor plan between rooms. Where there are doors, they are pocketed into the depth of the wall and seem to disappear, creating a sense of spaciousness that defies the old house stereotype of small cramped rooms. The interiors are drenched in sunlight drawn in through oversize windows. French doors open the formal parlors to the screen porch, adding an outdoor room to the sense of space. The windows and French doors have slender mullions that divide the glass into large panes, producing pro-

portions that are intentionally overscaled in Greek Revival designs.

In the most dramatic change to the traditional Greek Revival floor plan, the formal stair is turned around to ascend to the second floor from the back door rather than from the front hall. By reversing the stair, Gil created a more enclosed front vestibule and closed off views to second-floor bedrooms for more privacy. Doorways connecting the front entry hall to the stair, parlors, and kitchen wing make the vestibule a pivotal space.

A delicate vine-covered pergola, or arbor of lattice, supported by a pair of Doric columns, covers the back door. Criss-crossed layers of timbers create the lattice roof, which is cantilevered out beyond the columns on projecting beams. This refined structure showcases handcraftsmanship and authentic detailing.

Bonus Living Spaces

The screen porch is a bonus space that becomes a four-season outdoor living room when glass panels replace the screens in the winter (shown on page 102). The room looks like an open porch that was enclosed with screens in the late nineteenth century. Leftover details create the renovated look, because the painted clapboard siding and dark green louvered shutters of the "old" wall are still visible inside the room.

The small wing on the side of the main house includes the kitchen and work rooms. It is countrified in character to create the fiction that this part

of the house was built first, with narrow beadboard paneling on the walls and wide painted pine floorboards. The large brick hearth and plain details of its mantelpiece suggest that the fireplace was once used for cooking. Gil designed the kitchen with this story of country informality to contrast with the high-styled Grecian details of the main house.

The house is a fictional account of an 1830s Greek Revival house, but it is also an architect's vision fully realized. Gil's story illustrates the value of thorough historical research, the pursuit of authenticity and proper scale, and the investment in period fittings when building a new old house.

The main stair rises from the back hall to the second-floor landing rather than from the entry hall. The stair's turned newel post and spindles and scroll-cut brackets are patterned after measured details of Greek Revival millwork.

PRESERVING
HISTORY

You don't always have to start from scratch to create a new old house. This well-preserved historic house, filled with traces of Southern history, was graceful but timeworn when the owners found it. Through two and a half centuries of occupants, this Maryland Tidewater plantation has been altered and extended with a new old guesthouse, creating a true story of change over time.

A cross hall runs the length of the new old guesthouse, joining the living room to the sitting room through the kitchen. Kitchen cabinets and wall panels are painted slate blue, a dusty gray colonial color that complements other traditional shades of sage green, khaki, and cream.

The new guesthouse has a long, steeply pitched gable roof punctuated by four dormers, and white weatherboard walls, all designed as a direct translation of the original plantation house.

ozens of structures have dotted the grounds during its long history, but only the plantation house—with its smokehouse, storerooms, and a diminutive office—survived. The new owners have devoted themselves to preserving the history of the old house and have carefully added new buildings designed with authentic Tidewater details.

To restore the main residence and add on to the property, the homeowners commissioned architects Outerbridge Horsey and Merle Thorpe. The architects' design included a new guesthouse, a three-car garage, and a small cottage. The homeowners' only request was that the additions look like a natural extension of the original architecture, because they wanted to safeguard the historic integrity of the plantation. Simple as their request may seem, this was no small challenge for Outerbridge and Merle to meet.

The architects realized that they would be building in a sensitive setting and needed to gather clues about the traditions of Tidewater building to *Respect the Character of Place*. They studied the shapes, building materials, and decorative details of the plantation's old buildings in search of the classic themes of Eastern Shore architecture. The precedents the architects uncovered would provide clear direction about how to build in an authentic way.

The architects shaped the story of the plantation with a new chapter of alterations. The new guesthouse looks as if it might have been an old tenant house that was renovated for a new use, and the small cottage is tucked away from the main house as slave quarters might have been. Guided by the owners' wish to preserve the traditions of the manor, the architects invented new additions that were built on the same themes of history.

DECIDING ON A HISTORIC STYLE

Outerbridge and Merle uncovered three stages in the history of the main house's growth. The original Tidewater plantation house, built in 1724, was joined by a formal brick Georgian manor house in 1790 and a Colonial Revival kitchen addition in 1927. The architects' challenge was to decide which period from this range of styles the new structures should mimic.

Since the house was part of a historic property, they realized they would need to add new buildings without compromising the traditional integrity of the house. After seeking advice from their colleagues in historic preservation, the architects decided that the

This historic Tidewater plantation is an eighteenth-century house, enlarged by additions throughout the following 200 years. The Maryland plantation house (right) was built in 1724, and the late Georgian brick house (left) was added in 1790.

hallmarks of style
A HISTORIC TIDEWATER PLANTATION

This home sits on a peninsula of land carved from the web of tidal rivers that forms the Eastern Shore of Maryland. It is a plantation house built by a wealthy gentleman farmer. The original plantation was planted in tobacco and other cash crops. Sited on the banks of the Miles River, it was linked to nearby market towns via the waterways that served as highways in colonial Maryland.

Typical of tidewater houses of the eighteenth century, the settler's house is a one-and-a-half-story wood-frame house with dormers set into a steeply pitched roof. The house is built on brick foundations made from clay dug on the property. A single-story porch with a shallow-pitched roof runs the full length of the front. The walls are sided with horizontal beaded boards and the double-hung windows are divided into multiple panes.

The minuscule law office is one of the original outbuildings. Details on this and other antique structures offered precedents of style on which the architects could base the new designs.

oldest portion of the house, from 1724, should define the character of any new buildings. The style of the original plantation house would be the guide for the new designs.

THE NEW GUESTHOUSE

The new guesthouse is built with many details drawn from early-eighteenth-century Tidewater architecture—a steeply pitched roof; tall, narrow dormers; wood-covered side walls; and brick chimneys. The new one-and-a-half-story building with attic bedrooms authentically reproduces these common details.

Planned like an outbuilding, set apart from the manor house, the guesthouse evokes an image of a historic tenant house that has been meticulously restored. Sitting low to the ground on handmade brick foundations, the side walls are sheathed in 10-in.-wide weatherboards, detailed like those on the old plantation house. This siding is made of smooth boards that are set flush rather than overlapping like clapboard siding.

Like the earliest section of this residence, the pitched roof of the new guesthouse is punctuated with a row of four dormers, which draw light and views into the attic bedrooms. The narrow dormers are just wide enough to accommodate a six-over-six colonial-style window and its trim molding, creating strong vertical features that contrast with the horizontal lines of the house. Weatherboards cover the sides of the dormers and are angled to follow the slope of the roof, a common eighteenth-century architectural detail.

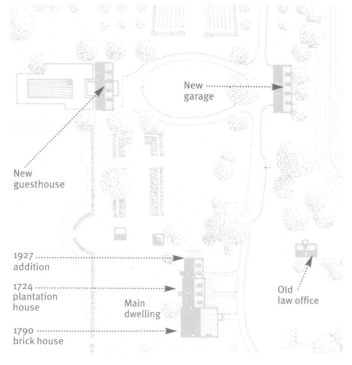

DATING THE PROPERTY

New guesthouse

New garage

1927 addition

1724 plantation house

1790 brick house

Main dwelling

Old law office

DORMERS, SHUTTERS, AND WEATHERBOARDS

→ The practical exterior woodwork of Tidewater plantation houses was enriched with subtle decorative details and shown here on the original plantation house. Walls of wide weatherboards are joined together edge to edge to form a smooth wall surface, and the horizontal joints between the boards are on their bottom edge. Molded trim surrounds each of the double-hung windows and sits on thick windowsills, shaped in a half-round profile, called a torus or bullnose. Window shutters—a functional feature used to seal out the cold—are made of raised panels rather than plain boards, which also would have done the job.

Dormers, embellished with woodworking details, are also essential design elements used to bring light and air into attic bedrooms. The dormers' steep-pitched roofs end in triangular pediments that are outlined with crown moldings to highlight the shape. Beaded weatherboards cover the dormer side walls and are set on an angle, following the slope of the roof. This distinctive way of cladding is a classic design feature in the Tidewater region.

Early Eastern Shore plantation houses often had porches supported by square posts and covered by shallow-pitched roofs that extended off the steep-pitched main roof. This type of roof, which changes pitch from steep to shallow, is called a cat-slide roof. The screen porch on the guesthouse is made to look like a traditional open porch that has been filled in with screen panels. On the front of the house, the small porch that extends over the main entrance is partially filled in with a band of casement windows that light the kitchen. These in-filled porches are designed to suggest renovations to an old house made at a later date, telling a story of changes over time.

A distinctive historical feature of a Southern Tidewater house is the brick end walls, like those on the new guesthouse. On old houses, masonry chim-

Like the open porches that are a historic feature on the Eastern Shore, the screen porch on the back of the guest house has a shallow roof supported by square posts.

In the guesthouse sitting room, the walls below the chair rail are finished with vertical beaded boards as in traditional wainscoting. The firebox is made of oversize handmade bricks, like the exterior end walls of the house. The lintel of splayed bricks that spans the fireplace opening is called a jack arch.

INTEGRATING MODERN COMFORTS

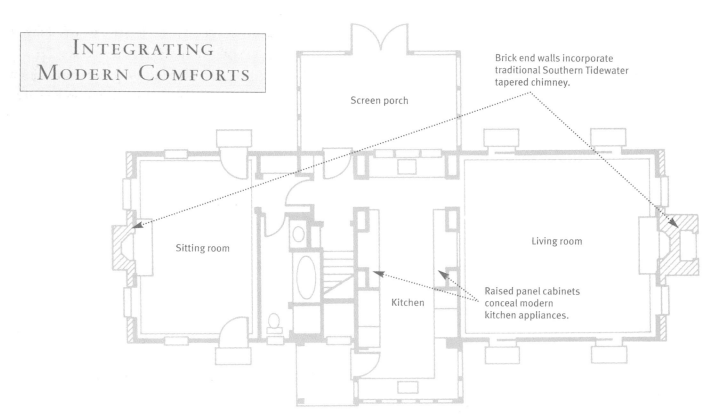

Brick end walls incorporate traditional Southern Tidewater tapered chimney.

Screen porch

Sitting room

Kitchen

Living room

Raised panel cabinets conceal modern kitchen appliances.

On the new guesthouse, a brick chimney has an outdoor grill designed into its base.

neys were built onto the outside of the walls in tapered stacks to disperse the heat of the fireplace. These brick ends were also a logical extension to the structural design, reinforcing the wooden frame of the house with solid masonry buttresses. The architects integrated an outdoor grill into the guesthouse's chimney stack, a new invention in keeping with the traditional style.

PERIOD INTERIORS

Outerbridge and Merle looked right next door to the original main house for ways to recreate the feel of period interiors in the new guesthouse. From the

The original winder stair in the 1724 plantation house (top) was the model for the new staircase in the cottage (bottom). The old stair, made of pie-shaped treads that wind around the newel post, is designed to take up the least possible floor space. The new stair is modified to meet modern building codes.

TRADITIONAL CRAFTSMANSHIP
PANELING A FIREPLACE WALL

➤ In an eighteenth-century Tidewater home, a wall of paneled woodwork around a fireplace was considered a stylish embellishment. The entire length of the fireplace wall was designed with beveled wooden panels set into frames to accent the importance of the fireplace. Cupboards were built into the recessed wall spaces around the chimney.

Modern paneled walls are made much as they were two centuries ago, except that the panels and frames are cut with molding machines rather than by hand. Measured drawings of eighteenth-century wall panels can serve as a design guide.

main house, they borrowed a wealth of inspiring historic details, including the fireplace wall of raised paneling, plain winder staircase, and simple beaded casing trim for the doors and windows. The floor plan of the guesthouse is laid out with a sitting room and a living room at the ends, separated by the kitchen and a staircase in the middle. A cross hall runs through the length of the house, connecting these two main rooms (shown on page 107).

The interior of the guesthouse looks far from old, however. Instead of entering a vestibule, the main entrance is a well-appointed modern kitchen that spans the width of the house. The walls are completely filled with raised-panel cabinets and old-fashioned frames, patterned after the panelling in the main house, giving the kitchen a traditional

flavor. But the granite countertops and stainless-steel appliances hidden by the kitchen cabinetry are clearly contemporary. The two styles may seem at odds, but the guesthouse is arranged to suit the needs of modern family living, made possible by *Incorporating Modern Conveniences* into traditional dress so that both work together seamlessly.

The raised-panel wall of the guesthouse living room is inspired by the paneling of the fireplace wall in the sitting room of the 1724 plantation house. The new wall is a composition of panels and frames of the simplest colonial design and surrounds a fireplace of handmade bricks. The wall of raised, slate blue panels is another authentic design element recalling the classic decorative woodwork on the fireplace walls of traditional Tidewater houses.

The woodwork in the sitting room parlor in the 1724 plantation house is a composition of simple raised panels that incorporates storage cupboard doors into the design. The fireplace bricks are covered with white gypsum plaster for a clean finish.

BRINGING
A FARM
BACK TO LIFE

Craig and Pat Ruppert found a forlorn-looking farm in the Maryland countryside that was nothing but cornfields. They set out to bring the old farm back to life with a new house that looks as if it had always been there. Versaci Neumann & Partners, my architecture firm, created an authentic farmhouse that duplicated the building traditions of mid-eighteenth-century Maryland.

The German stone farmhouse sits on the brow of a hill of old oaks, overlooking a pond. Located on a farm with no preserved historic house, the new stone house is meant to look like an eighteenth-century original, meticulously restored for modern living.

The new stone farmhouse, surrounded by open fields, is nestled on the crest of a hill that overlooks a new pond carved out of the boggy bottomland. From its hillside perch, the house has commanding views of the farm and looks aged and weathered in place, yet with the fresh demeanor of a house recently restored. Furthermore, the house appears as if generations of renovations had taken place over a long period of time. To create this new old house, we studied the local building traditions for clues to the traditional details and techniques used by eighteenth-century German builders. Discovering the way old farmhouses sit on the lay of the land, we sited the new house so it was settled in on a natural saddle of ground. There, the house looks right at home because it *Respects the Character of Place* by working with the features of the property.

A RENOVATED LOOK

Although the Rupperts wanted to build an authentic farmhouse, they also wanted the house to meet the pragmatic needs of their daily lives. So the house has a livable plan adjusted to the everyday routine of their young family, without sacrificing elements of historic detail that make the house feel genuine. Within a classic center hall plan (a traditional farmhouse layout), new spaces and new functions accommodate modern living. For instance, there is an ample kitchen with pantry space and a mudroom full of storage cupboards. It appears as if an old house were thoughtfully remodeled on the inside over a number of years.

While the plan of the farmhouse is updated, there are finish details throughout the interiors that preserve the period tradition. Profiles for authentic trim moldings, chair rails, and stair parts were developed from measured drawings of eighteenth-century millwork in our library of historic architecture. We chose elements that were traditionally used by German builders in the Mid-Atlantic colonies. Details of period woodwork add subtle notes of tradition to rooms that function in contemporary ways, creating the look of a sensitive renovation to an older home.

CREATING FICTIONAL HISTORY

In the fabricated story of the farmhouse, there are four chapters, each representing an imaginary period of building history. As typical farmhouses evolved over generations, the materials used for building

Fieldstone chimneys tie together several generations of buildings with different exterior materials. The stucco wing is attached to the stone house like an early-eighteenth-century cabin, and the guesthouse, with clapboard siding, looks like a nineteenth-century summer kitchen.

In the make-believe history of the house, the breezeway connecting the house to the summer kitchen (now the guesthouse) has been enclosed. The exterior clapboard walls and the flagstone floor give the appearance of a remodeled porch.

Two pairs of French doors open the stair hall to the double parlor, which is the living room and dining room. The wide framed door openings, although not historically authentic, bring more light into the hall and allow the parlor to be closed off.

Period woodwork adds tradition
to rooms that function in modern ways,
creating the look of a sensitive
renovation to an older home.

walls and roofs and the finish details for cornices and trims changed with the times. New construction materials, such as stucco, stud walls, and metal roofs, replaced the older, more labor intensive construction, such as fieldstone and timber frame. These changes often date each section to a historic time frame, such as early eighteenth century or post Civil War. This farmhouse sets out to recreate several building periods, separated in time by detailing each structure with materials that are authentic to a historic period.

The story of the farmhouse begins with the main house made of fieldstone. It is attached to a one-story stucco wing, which was designed to look like an original timber-frame cabin. The third section, the former summer kitchen, sided in ochre-colored clapboard, is now a guesthouse, connected to the main house by a glassed-in breezeway. Across from the guesthouse is the fourth structure, a carriage barn garage covered in painted clapboard that looks like the last old outbuilding on the farm. Together these four structures look as if they exist to tell a story of accumulated additions that took years to build.

hallmarks of style
GERMAN STONE FARMHOUSE

German farmers from Pennsylvania migrated to upland Maryland and Virginia in the mid-eighteenth century in search of fertile land. They followed the mountains south from Lancaster and Bucks Counties into the Southern Piedmont, bringing their farming and building traditions with them. These farmers built simple, sturdy houses and barns constructed of fieldstone and oak timbers using Old-World methods.

The vernacular stone houses of the Pennsylvania German builders were plain rectangular structures made of roughly coursed blocks of fieldstone laid up in a random pattern. The steep roofs were framed in sturdy oak timbers and covered with hand-split wood shingles.

Houses were often built into a hill to keep the lower floor cool, a style called a bank house. Windows were arranged in even rows framed by board-and-batten or raised-panel shutters. Later, Georgian designs were adapted to make the facades more symmetrical.

A dogleg staircase is recessed into the wall. The antique heart pine floors, with knots, mineral stains, and nail holes, impart the patina of age.

teristic German stonework is laid in a random pattern of interlaced stones and mortar joints that animate the simple shape of the house.

NEW OLD OUTBUILDINGS

The guesthouse and carriage barn garage are clapboard outbuildings that are nineteenth-century additions to the story of the farm. Built of wooden stud wall construction and finished with lapped siding, the guesthouse might have been a summer kitchen that was renovated for a new use. Its fieldstone chimney appears to be a remnant from an earlier building, which may have burned down; but the walls, covered in German-board siding, date the guesthouse to the mid-nineteenth century. The painted standing-seam metal roof was not commonly used until the railroads made the material widely available after 1870. Metal roofs on the porches and breezeway, as well as on the carriage barn garage, date their construction to this same time period.

TWO FRONT PORCHES

The farmhouse is designed to have two fronts, one overlooking the pond and fields and the other facing the entrance drive. The idea began with the Rupperts' desire for a view through the center of the house, as in a classic Georgian manor. They wanted doorways that lined up in the middle of

THE MAIN HOUSE

The main house is built of local fieldstones harvested from old walls in western Pennsylvania, which makes the structure look as if it were built around 1750. The house is composed in a simple country Georgian style, defined by a symmetrical facade of five windows across the front and a center hall plan. Windows are boldly framed in wide trim moldings from the Georgian period (1720–1790). The charac-

each facade so that they could see straight through to the pond and rolling landscape beyond.

Porches often embellish Maryland's eighteenth-century stone houses. Many were added after the Civil War to shelter the entrance or to be used as an elegant design upgrade. Here, the front porch, with its plain shed roof on square wooden posts, forms a simple portico (shown on page 126). On the pond front, the sitting porch takes in the view of the land. Its wooden posts are detailed with base and crown moldings in a loose interpretation of a classical column, a form that was traditional for the era (shown on page 127).

In the updated floor plan, the formal rooms are combined in a double parlor, which serves as living room and dining room. The raised-panel mantelpiece wall, Georgian-style window casings, and chair rail provide traditional details.

The family room and sun porch have been joined together, as if they were remodeled, leaving only the structural posts in place. The former outside walls of the sun porch have been filled in with pairs of double-hung windows set between the old porch posts. The sun-drenched room is used for informal dining and extra family room space.

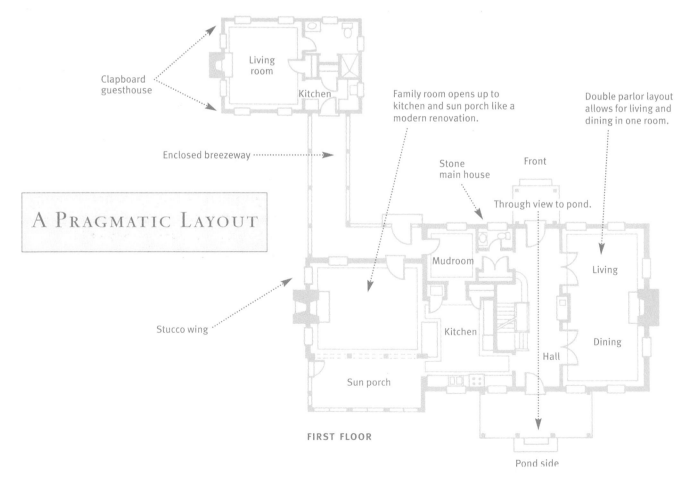

A Pragmatic Layout

Clapboard guesthouse

Living room

Kitchen

Family room opens up to kitchen and sun porch like a modern renovation.

Double parlor layout allows for living and dining in one room.

Enclosed breezeway

Stone main house

Front

Through view to pond.

Mudroom

Living

Stucco wing

Kitchen

Dining

Hall

Sun porch

FIRST FLOOR

Pond side

The broad opening between rooms
is a contemporary way to join spaces
in an open plan, as is often done
when old houses are renovated.

INTERIORS FOR
TODAY'S LIFESTYLE

Though the exteriors strive for period authenticity, the interior floor plan is designed for the needs of a busy modern family. The front door is placed in the center of the facade, leading guests into a wide stair hall that looks like the classic layout of a center hall house. We rearranged the traditional floor plan laid out with four rooms that open from the stair hall to suit new living patterns, as if the old farmhouse had been completely renovated to *Incorporate Modern Conveniences.*

The living room and dining areas are combined into one large formal room, filling one end of the house with a double parlor. Pairs of French doors close the room from the stair hall, creating a private space that the family uses for music practice. Across the central hall, the kitchen fills another corner of the floor plan and is big enough to allow friends to pull up stools under a table-size island. Filled with cabinets, counters, and a pantry wall, this modern kitchen bears no resemblance to an eighteenth-century farmhouse kitchen, which would have been in the cellar or, more often, in a separate outbuilding. The last corner of the plan is a spacious mudroom with storage lockers for each child, clearly planned to accommodate the comings and goings of a large family.

Antique barn beams frame the ceiling of the family room, located in the stucco wing. The room is designed to look like a renovated eighteenth-century structure cleared to expose the timber frame. A massive stone fireplace on the end wall is built with the same Pennsylvania fieldstone as the exterior walls.

A gravel parking court in front of the farmhouse is a modern landscape feature. The unusually shaped clapboards on the guesthouse, with a cove cut in the top edge, is called German-board siding. It is commonly used throughout the Piedmont, thought to be introduced by early German settlers.

TRADITIONAL CRAFTSMANSHIP

FIELDSTONE AND LIME MORTAR

→ Fieldstones salvaged from old walls in western Pennsylvania are laid in random layers, called uncoursed rubble. The setting mortar imitates the color and texture of the traditional soft lime mortars used in eighteenth-century construction—a mixture of white Portland cement, slaked lime, and coarse brown construction sand.

The joints between stones are tuck pointed (tightly packed with mortar) and then struck (finished) with a raised V-shaped joint that projects out from the stones. Old-time masons used this joint to shed rainwater and protect the soft lime. The new mortar was aged, to make

the joints look weathered over decades, by washing the wall with acid to burn the lime to tan and by hosing down the mortar to expose the grains of brown sand. Nature has added to the aging process by leaching a brown iron oxide film of rust across the fieldstones.

The fieldstone house resembles the eighteenth-century foursquare farmhouses built by Pennsylvania German farmers who migrated to Maryland's fertile lands. Its sturdy, austere look recalls the straightforward German building tradition.

The kitchen leads into the family room and the stucco wing, where a 10-ft.-wide passage cut through the stone wall of the main house connects the two rooms. The broad opening between rooms is a contemporary way to join spaces in an open plan, as is often done when old houses are renovated. Within the vaulted interior space of the family room, timber trusses span from wall to wall, supporting a high ceiling (shown on page 125). The exposed antique ceiling beams are meant to simulate the heavy timbers that frame the stucco wing,

although this section is actually built with wood stud walls.

In the make-believe story of renovations, one of the exterior walls of the family room wing was removed to open into a sun porch, leaving only the structural posts that supported the old wall. Although this story of changes is a fabrication, many of the reworked details are consciously designed to imitate the results of contemporary remodeling that opened up an old-fashioned floor plan.

A HOUSE
OF
SALVAGED BONES

It takes an artist's eye to assimilate antique materials and finishes into a new house so the look of age is convincingly authentic. Done by inexperienced hands without the vision for traditional forms, the combination of salvaged materials and reproduction fittings with new finish details can easily look clumsy and cobbled together.

The interior of this new old Cape Cod house has a light touch of Federal period detailing rather than heavy panel moldings of the earlier Georgian style. The door and window frames are simple pilaster-style casings.

John and Ginger Laytham recreated a classic Cape Cod cottage by hiring Gregory Schipa, a designer and builder with a historian's eye for detail, honed by years of working on restorations. Although the house is not a restoration, the casual observer could easily be fooled. Greg blended new architectural details with antique building parts inside and out to create an authentic reproduction of a Cape Cod house, finished in the Greek Revival style that was popular in New England from 1820 to 1850.

The framework is a post-and-beam timber frame pulled from an 1836 Cape Cod–style house the builder dismantled in Vermont. Greg combined the Vermont structure with the timber frame of an old Nantucket fisherman's cottage to create an L-shaped wing for the Cape. But the foundations and wall finishes are new work crafted with authentic accuracy. The custom moldings and trimwork were fabricated with historic profiles and dimensions to match vintage fittings. As a result, the new house looks as if it had aged gracefully, because it is built with a blend of reproduction and salvaged materials.

A CLASSICAL COTTAGE SURPRISE

Though Nantucket is famous for its weathered shingle cottages from the early colonial days, the Laythams' recreated house dates to the beginning of the nineteenth century, when whaling brought prosperity to the island. Early cottages with simple unadorned shapes and sober shingle exteriors were later refined with the classical details of the Federal and Greek Revival styles, a historic architectural evolution reflected in this new old house.

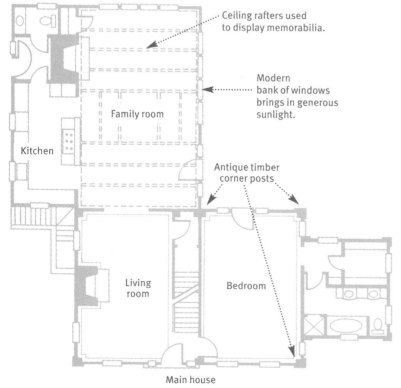

A VINTAGE
FRAMEWORK

Ceiling rafters used to display memorabilia.

Modern bank of windows brings in generous sunlight.

Family room

Kitchen

Antique timber corner posts

Living room

Bedroom

Main house

FIRST FLOOR

The new Cape Cod has a straightforward gable shape and a pitched roof without dormers. The white-painted facade is a hallmark of the Greek Revival style.

The traditional parlor is designed with Federal-style trimwork, a decorative style that continued to be used in the interiors of later Greek Revival houses. Unlike a traditional Cape, the staircase and doorway open to the parlor, a modern design that brightens and enlarges the front room.

Recycled pine floorboards, recovered from old New England buildings, cloak the rooms with a persuasive patina of age.

While the house is still considered a Cape, because it maintains the traditional story-and-a-half shape, the new house is a classical surprise. It is decorated in Greek Revival style, with some details that are new reproductions and others that are saved from an old Vermont house (circa 1836). Almost all of the elegant millwork patterns have been reproduced from remnants of the Vermont house. The vintage timber frames are wrapped in authentic Greek Revival details that look as if they dated back to the 1830s. These classical elements, painted white, are hallmarks of the Greek Revival style. White

The front facade of the guest cottage is covered in painted clapboards and has a decorative door surround. The gable ends are simple weathered shingles, dating the look of the cottage to the mid-1700s.

became the color of choice for New England houses after the Greek Revival took hold in the 1820s. In keeping with history, the new house is painted white to symbolize purity of character, a traditional virtue expressed in the style.

The front door's surround is elaborately framed by a pair of classical square columns that support a frieze and cornice. Classical pilasters wrap each corner

The antique front door in the entry vestibule was salvaged from an early nineteenth-century Vermont house. The painted green-black door has deep panel moldings and delicate multi-paned sidelights typical of the Greek Revival period.

of the facade, and a wide frieze band runs across the front above the pilasters.

A Traditional Back Ell

Though the facade appears symmetrical, it is actually unbalanced, with two windows on one side of the front door and only one on the other. This renders the cottage a three-quarter Cape, rather than a full Cape, which would have balanced pairs of windows. Many early cottages started out as a half Cape, with an off-center front door and two windows, but over

The Cape Cod style developed from the simple one-and-a-half-story colonial houses of eighteenth-century coastal New England. These houses were built by English settlers in a hall-and-parlor layout around a massive center chimney.

The earliest houses were covered with wattle and daub and thatched roofs, but the settlers soon discovered that hand-split wood shingles were more durable and versatile. As colonists prospered, they added two bedchambers above and then a lean-to addition out the back for a kitchen and larder, creating the New England saltbox.

By 1800, these colonial houses became known as Cape Cod cottages. The Cape-style house is distinctive because of its lack of ornamentation; plain boxed cornice; squared window heads; a door surround made of flat, square-cut boards, and naturally weathered shingles. Some later houses were sided with formal clapboard. A Cape embellished with classical details takes on the characteristics of the Georgian or Greek Revival style.

Inside the guest cottage, comfortable colonial period rooms are created with antique materials gathered from around New England, including wide plank floors, hewn ceiling beams, and walls of old wood paneling.

CLASSICAL ENTRANCE PORTICO

➤An elegantly wrought classical entrance portico is the signature feature of this Greek Revival–style Cape house. The millwork details are reproduced of an original portico from an 1836 Vermont house. The portico is a framed doorway that surrounds the front door, also called a frontispiece, and is composed of classical parts that simulate columns that hold up a horizontal frieze and cornice. Set in high relief against the clapboard wall, the sides of the portico are square Doric pilaster columns with faces that are fluted, or grooved. The original front door and sidelights from the Vermont house are incorporated into the new portico. Delicate muntins, or wooden grilles, divide the panes of the two sidelights and companion transom window that surrounds the front door.

time, they were extended in length to double the size of the house. Wings were often added off the backs of Capes to add depth to the house, forming a traditional kitchen ell.

The back ell of this house closely fits the classic image of a shingled Nantucket home. There are almost no decorative details on the exterior walls, which are covered in weathered pine shingles, except for simple flat corner boards and window trim painted white. The shingled walls and roof express the taut and spare look of early New England frugality.

The Greek Revival front and shingled back ell look as if they had settled into the property over

Finely crafted wooden moldings, which reproduce traditional profiles, decorate the corners of the house. In this detail, a square pilaster column anchored to the corner of the house supports the triangular cornice return. Deeply carved profiles accent the otherwise simple shapes of the moldings.

An antique mantelpiece brought from a New England Federal period house surrounds the fireplace. The dusty hue of the painted khaki woodwork gives the room a colonial cast.

have had a vestibule as a buffer to keep cold air from the rest of the house. In this house, the vestibule is opened up to make the parlor spacious.

A COMPANION COTTAGE

A guest cottage was built across the front walk from the main house (shown on page 132). Although it is new on the outside, the cottage's interior is finished with salvaged antique parts for the floors, walls, ceiling beams, doors, and hardware.

The molding profiles of the cottage's facade are simplified in keeping with the structure's secondary importance. The white-painted clapboard front and weathered shingle sides and back offer an example of how early-eighteenth-century New England houses looked. Often, early homes were unadorned, built by struggling colonists who had no time for ornament. Once settlers prospered, they embellished the front of their main homes, leaving the rest plain.

Antique materials woven into the construction of the cottage's parlor simulate an authentic interior (shown on page 134). Old square-hewn barn beams form the ceiling, and the fireplace wall is paneled in vertical boards with the original timeworn slate blue milk paint still intact. Period details that create a convincing portrait of an authentic colonial interior include the flat-panel doors with their cast-iron thumb latches.

many years, convincing some Nantucket natives that the house is historic.

A SPACIOUS ENTRY

Once across the granite threshold and through the dark green black paneled front door, visitors are immediately struck by the beauty and authenticity of the floors. Recycled pine floorboards, recovered from old New England buildings, cloak the rooms with a persuasive patina of age. The aged boards are the color of amber—some 12 in. to 15 in. wide, with a curiously gnarly texture, and their faces are pocked with worm tracks left long ago.

The front door of the main cottage opens directly into the living room parlor instead of into a foyer (shown on page 131). An original Cape would

Timber framing is the classic structure for a barn, but the same methods were used for house framing through the mid-nineteenth century. Two bedrooms fit in the attic, where traces of the old post-and-beam frame have been left exposed.

A NEW FARMHOUSE
FOR AN OLD VILLAGE

When you are faced with building a new house in a historic landmark town with strict preservation codes, there is only one thing to do. Build a house that is tailor made for the village by blending it into the existing landscape while incorporating authentic details of the local building tradition into the architecture.

The style of this new old house is based on the early-nineteenth-century houses in the town. Period detailing and traditional materials, like fieldstone foundations and a tin roof, make the house comfortably fit the neighborhood like a well-worn shoe.

Bathed in sunlight, moldings, window frames, and porch posts cast strong shadows that highlight the architectural details. Moldings carved in high relief outline the parts with crisp edges.

My firm started by studying the character of the town where the new house would be built, looking for historic clues to the area's building traditions. By *Respecting the Character of Place,* we intended to make the new old house complement its setting by closely matching, but not necessarily copying, the materials and styles of the older houses. The historic elements of the local style became our creative springboard for a new design. This farmhouse shows how a new home can mingle in a town filled with antique houses by respecting its neighbors.

Many new traditional-style houses built in old towns look inauthentic because they lack the accurate period details and materials that give vintage homes their visual interest and depth. This new old farmhouse is steeped in local character, because it is brimming with authentic period details for porches, dormers, clapboards, and moldings.

The house sits on a hillside site in a historic landmark village nestled in the foothills of Virginia's Blue Ridge Mountains. If it weren't for the paved roads and overhead power lines, this village, settled

TRADITIONAL CRAFTSMANSHIP
CLASSIC TIN ROOF

➤Classic tin roofs that once graced old houses from the Mid-Atlantic through the Old South are being rediscovered for new old houses. A tin roof is made up of metal sheets, about 17 in. wide, formed into pans on the ground with their long edges turned up about 1½ in. high. On the roof, two pans are placed side by side, and their edges are then folded together, or crimped, to make watertight, closed running joints called standing seams. While the roof on this farm-

house is made of copper sheets, rather than the traditional tin-coated steel, the durability and rich patina of this material is a better investment. The copper will last more than 50 years without painting and is more flexible than steel through temperature changes.

The spacious front porch features painted floorboards, beadboard ceiling, square post, and picket railings. It is a classic nineteenth-century Virginia porch that invites visitors to put up their feet and set a spell.

by Quakers in 1733, would look much like it did 100 years ago. The local preservation foundation works diligently to keep it that way, and this new Piedmont farmhouse passes the town's stringent test.

A DISTINCTIVE SILHOUETTE

The design of the house is one and a half stories tall (a floor with dormer windows counts as a half story), a simple gable on a stone foundation with a roof interrupted by dormers. The roofline of punched dormers, or half dormers partially embedded in the walls, makes the house appear to be a sin-

The new farmhouse is a recreated vintage shell that incorporates the conveniences of modern living.

gle story and an appropriately modest size and height in a village of old homes. Half dormers sit low on the roof and are visually less intrusive against the town's bucolic backdrop. We adapted the idea for these dormers from traditional English cottages, an old architectural trick not usually seen on local

Many Southern Piedmont farmhouses were painted bright white at the turn of the last century, when white lead and linseed oil paint was the most practical, durable finish. Windows are grouped in an orderly symmetry that would have appealed to the straightforward thinking of the area's Quaker settlers.

ARCHITECTURAL DETAILS
D O R M E R S

Though the punched dormers on this new old house may look unusual, they share many characteristics common to this most distinctive roof feature. Dormers are a clever invention for bringing daylight through the roof and to brighten attic bedrooms with natural light. Set onto the front edge of the roof in groups of two to five, dormers create a lively pattern of rhythmically spaced architectural elements.

Dormers have taken many shapes in history, but the doghouse form is the most common one on American homes. They can be found in many shapes on traditional house styles, from simple gables on Greek Revival houses to shed dormers on Craftsman bungalows. Wherever dormers are used, they should be placed in a regular, rhythmic pattern that is synchronized with the spacing of the windows. To be historically correct, make sure dormers are not applied haphazardly or placed in random locations.

MODERN FAMILY FARMHOUSE

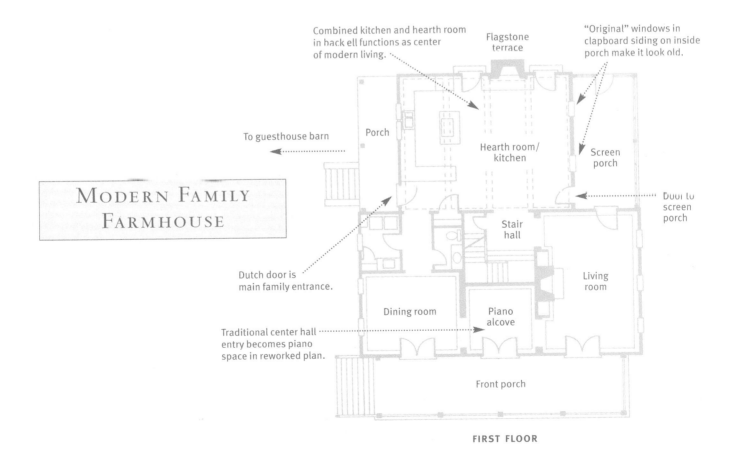

Combined kitchen and hearth room in back ell functions as center of modern living.

Flagstone terrace

"Original" windows in clapboard siding on inside porch make it look old.

To guesthouse barn

Porch

Hearth room/ kitchen

Screen porch

Door to screen porch

Stair hall

Living room

Dutch door is main family entrance.

Dining room

Piano alcove

Traditional center hall entry becomes piano space in reworked plan.

Front porch

FIRST FLOOR

homes, where the fully exposed rooftop dormer is
more typical. But they illustrate an example of
Inventing within the Rules by configuring an old element of style in a new way.

SOUTHERN PIEDMONT FARMHOUSE

The Southern Piedmont farmhouses of
rural Virginia provided a source of architectural details to make this new old
house fit into its well-preserved town. These
historic houses are center hall farmhouses decorated with stylish details from the Georgian,
Greek Revival, and Victorian periods.

The typical local house is a simple two-
story gable braced at each end by a chimney,
with a symmetrical pattern of windows across
the front and a prominent raised front porch.
The sturdy front porches were built with simple classical columns or turned posts with Victorian brackets. The main part of the house
runs parallel to the street, and an attached perpendicular rear wing extends out the back.
Houses have exposed fieldstone foundation
walls, clapboard siding, a painted standing-
seam tin roof, and grouped dormers. Other
common details include shutters, corner
boards, and crisply worked cornices.

ROOF WITH A WEATHERED PATINA

The distinctive tin roof is a classic feature on the
new farmhouse, called a tin roof because of its
resemblance to a tin can. Years ago, a traditional tin
roof was made of metal sheets coated with tin that
were formed with turned-up edges, called standing
seams. This new roof is made of copper sheets that
have weathered quickly to a ruddy brown color and
in time will acquire the familiar green patina of aged
copper. Although the use of copper is not historically correct, because it was rare and quite expensive at
the turn of the last century, it is used now instead of
steel because it is more durable and never needs
painting. The butterfly castings attached to the base
of the seams are called snow guards, used to keep
snow from sliding off the roof in dangerously heavy
sheets (shown on page 143).

BRINGING PLAIN WALLS TO LIFE

A strong projecting cornice, or roof edge, is a char-
acteristic of old houses built out to protect the walls
of the house from falling rain. Also designed to accent
the horizontal line of the eaves, the cornice is composed of layers of carved moldings that overhang the
wall by more than 1 ft. The dramatic overhang marks
a sharp visual distinction between the wall plane and
the roof and carves a strong silhouette against the sky.

Creating patterns of light and dark that play
across the textures of a wall is a traditional design
tool that brings plain walls to life. Strong sunlight
creates shadows that collect in the three-dimensional
details of decorative moldings. Seen in full daylight,
trim moldings shaped in bold relief around doors,

In keeping with the simple farmhouse theme of the interiors, kitchen cabinets are detailed in Quaker-plain cherrywood with oiled soapstone countertops. The kitchen is at the heart of the house; it adjoins the hearth room to make one large family living space that accommodates a contemporary lifestyle.

Formal rooms across the front of the house are joined together through wide doorways, with the piano alcove in the center. Natural light floods the interior rooms, highlighting the patina of the antique heart pine floors.

windows, and building corners highlight the special features of the design. The sculpted moldings add depth to the house facade and outline the pattern of openings in the wall. Similarly, the thick edges of beveled clapboard siding reinforce the texture of the wall by casting a regular pattern of shadow lines. These are powerful design elements that can be readily used to add texture to a new old house.

A MEMORABLE FIRST IMPRESSION

The prominent front porch stretches across the length of the house to make a strong first impression. As the formal centerpiece of the design, the porch becomes the ceremonial front door in the same way that a welcoming porch on an old house invites you to come on in. At 10 ft. wide and 40 ft. long, the porch conveys an image of the archetypal Southern farmhouse. It is an expansive outdoor gathering place that sits a full story above the ground, supported by stone piers that anchor the house to the site. The fieldstone piers are a reminder of the tradition of stone building brought to the town by Quakers in the early eighteenth century and used as a common foundation material on old houses (shown on page 138).

RETHINKING THE HALL AND PARLOR

The interior of a traditional Southern Piedmont farmhouse was typically organized in a center hall-and-parlor plan. A central stair hall divided the house into two major rooms—a hall that combined family living and dining and a parlor of fine furniture and collectibles reserved for guests. But we reshaped the traditional floor plan layout for the new old farmhouse, taking liberties with tradition that accommodate the needs of a contemporary lifestyle. The new farmhouse is a recreated vintage shell that incorporates the conveniences of modern living.

The pair of French doors, with transom windows above, is a design element borrowed from the tradition of verandas on French Colonial plantation houses—an example of creatively adapting forms from another style.

The stair hall, now placed in the middle of the house, is enclosed by walls, and the rest of the living spaces flow around it. The traditional entry vestibule is converted into an alcove designed to accommodate a baby grand piano. Placed to either side of the alcove, the living room and dining room fill out the front areas of the house. These rooms connect to each other through wide framed doorways, and each room opens out to the front porch through paired French doors. By opening to the porch, the interior rooms extend to the outdoors and capture the best views of the town.

The centerpiece of the hearth room is a large Rumford fireplace raised above the floor with a flagstone bench as the hearthstone. In the nineteenth century, England's Count Rumford perfected a firebox design of shallow depth with sharply angled side walls to throw more heat from the fire, a design now favored by traditional architects.

THE HEART OF THE HOUSE

Today, the new locus of family life is not in the parlor but in the kitchen, where daily living occurs around the breakfast table, and in the family room. As in olden times, the kitchen and hearth are the center of this contemporary family's activities. It is possible to incorporate the modern lifestyle changes into a new old house by reshaping the floor plan to include new functions that are built within old-looking additions, like a wing or back ell.

In this farmhouse, a spacious wing with low porches is attached to the back of the house, like an old-fashioned ell containing the kitchen and hearth room. The real family entrance to the house is through a Dutch door that leads into the kitchen from a side porch. Once inside, it is clear that the heart of the house is here, where the family connects to cook and dine.

The kitchen and hearth room are combined into one large space, focused on a brick-and-stone Rumford fireplace. The extrawide hearthstone provides a seating bench for family gatherings.

THE ILLUSION OF AN OLD PORCH

The screen porch, located off of the kitchen and hearth room, looks like a nineteenth-century addition that was screened in at a later date.

To reinforce the illusion of a remodeled porch, the interior walls are covered in painted clapboard siding with the "old" windows still in place; the porch posts are visible in the corners, holding up the screen panels. The porch ceiling is finished in old-fashioned painted beadboard paneling, but modern skylights pierce the boards to bring in more daylight. Despite these modern-looking intrusions, the porch retains the illusion of times gone by.

The back porch is a new outdoor room built to reproduce the image of an old porch addition later enclosed with screen panels. The windows and clapboard siding on the interior walls are meant to look like remnants from before the porch was added on, while the skylights that pierce the old-fashioned beadboard ceiling look like recent renovations.

PROPER

SOUTHERN MANNERS

The white-pillared plantation houses of the Old South were designed to be impressive. Rows of classical columns surrounded mansions built from 1820 to 1860, when fortunes were made from cultivating rice, sugar, and cotton. Greek Revival houses, with their wooden columns, mimicked ancient temples.

The view through the living room door crosses the veranda along the brick path down to the river. This Greek Revival–style house is shrouded in mature oak trees and tall cedars, making it look settled into the land.

Southern plantations were meant to be impressive when seen from the rivers that were the principal highways of the nineteenth-century South. This stately facade is created by wooden classical columns, designed to resemble a Greek temple. The new old white-pillared plantation house is perfectly symmetrical, with a veranda carved out of the center on two floors of its long facade.

This new plantation house, designed by architect Jim Strickland, recreates an authentic Greek Revival plantation house. This style features tall classical columns and a deep cornice beam, called a frieze, that define the facades, making the house instantly recognizable as a Southern antebellum plantation. Although it is not a copy of a historic house, every detail is *Invented within the Rules* of style to make the house look genuine. And only the best materials were used to construct this new old house, which is built to last. The time-tested materials and Old World construction methods chosen by the architect ensure that this house is *Built for the Ages.*

THE IMPORTANCE OF COLUMNS

The main feature of the house's exterior is a row of two-story columns that divide up the facade to look like the image of a Greek temple. The 24-ft.-tall columns are designed in the Greek Doric order—one of the three column systems of ancient Greek architecture that regulates proportions (see "Greek Revival Columns" on page 154). Jim used the Doric order as a guide to control the size of columns, the height of the cornice, and the proportions of windows and doors as he invented his new old house.

The Greek Doric columns are completely round in the center of the facade, and there are square pilasters at the corners, capped by a simple Doric cornice and frieze that trim the edge of the roof. Authentic classical moldings in bold shapes outline the important features of the facades, and these Greek Revival details stand out as they cast strong shadows in sunlight. In the plantation house tradition, the walls are painted bright white to symbolize the purity of a Greek temple. The only colorful decorative element that contrasts with the white walls is found in the green black wooden shutters on the ground floor.

THE VIEW FROM THE RIVER ROAD

In the 1800s, tidewater rivers were the major highways between Southern plantation houses in coastal Georgia, and the comings and goings of visitors and

A gracious stairway glides between Greek Doric columns to the main living floor. The columns support a cornice and frieze, called an entablature, which runs beneath the edge of the roof. These details recreate the design of a Greek Revival antebellum plantation.

Lower-level floors and walls are made of brick to resist damage from flooding. The stucco plaster over brick is made to look decayed to mimic the condition of an old plantation basement.

ARCHITECTURAL DETAILS
GREEK REVIVAL COLUMNS

The columns of this new old house are made in the Greek Doric order, one of the three principal column types of ancient Greece: Doric, Ionic, and Corinthian. Each of the three orders is defined by the details of its column capital, shaft, and base. The Greek Doric is the least elaborate of the three, composed of a round pillow-shaped capital, a fluted column shaft, and no base. The Doric column is designed to signify sturdy simplicity. By contrast, the refined Ionic capital curls into ram's horns (volutes) at the corners, and the fanciful Corinthian capital sprouts acanthus leaves around its vaselike shape.

DORIC   IONIC   CORINTHIAN

the flow of trade occurred on the water. The view of the house from the river side was as important as that from the land side. Following tradition, the new house is a symmetrical design in which the gracious river facade mirrors the front facade, with the same range of columns and a grand staircase. This new old house is an almost perfect square plan, following the pattern of many of the old plantations, which were as deep as they were wide.

Since the second floor is the primary living floor, a grand central staircase sweeps up between the round columns to a broad covered porch that leads to the front door. Covered porches, or verandas, are carved out of the center of the house on both the river and the land sides, and these gracious verandas are congenial gathering places. The porch ceilings are finished with shallow coffers, or wooden panels framed between rows of thin boards, all

The second-story veranda is a hallmark of the Southern plantation, designed as an outdoor gathering place to catch cooling breezes. The passage into the living room is marked by a diminutive pair of Doric columns.

Details of an old-fashioned kitchen include flat-panel cabinets resembling turn-of-the-last-century kitchen furniture. The cabinets are aged with a gray patina over cream paint. The ceramic farmhouse sink and soapstone counters create a warm, casual workspace.

CENTRAL LIVING SPACE

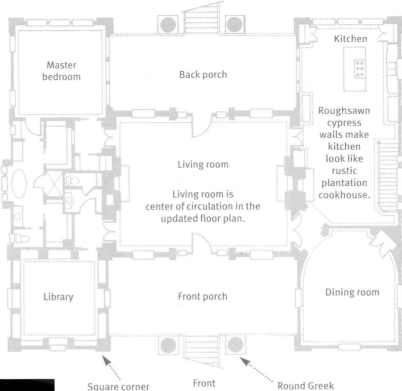

River side

Master bedroom

Back porch

Kitchen

Roughsawn cypress walls make kitchen look like rustic plantation cookhouse.

Living room

Living room is center of circulation in the updated floor plan.

MAIN FLOOR

Library

Front porch

Dining room

Square corner pilaster columns

Front

Round Greek Doric columns

View straight through house focuses on river.

The sash frames of the kitchen windows are finished with gray over cream paint, which takes the freshly minted edge off the new woodwork.

painted white. This ceiling pattern is common on old coastal houses, because the panels offer a durable and decorative covering in the moist climate.

PLANNED FOR TIDEWATER WEATHER

In the traditional architecture of Tidewater Georgia, there was good reason to raise the main floor a full story above ground, explaining the layout of this new plantation. The damp soils and frequent tidal floods of the coastal plains made the level land unsuitable for finely finished living spaces. The ground floors of the old plantations were reserved for kitchens and storerooms, while the raised main floors held the formal living room, dining room, and bedrooms, where they were protected from flood waters and had better access to cooling breezes.

A WEATHERED BAYOU
COTTAGE

It is easy to see how residents of this Louisiana river town would mistake this new old house for an antique. The French Creole–style home looks so authentic that one elderly resident swears the house has been there since her childhood. The truth is that restoration builder Ron Arnoult recently built this house from scratch.

The galerie porch is a trademark of a French Creole cottage. French doors open rooms to the galerie, drawing in cool breezes. The slender porch posts, or colonettes, turned with a distinctive swell in the shaft, are a Creole tradition.

From the street, this house, in the tranquil riverfront town of Madisonville, looks settled in a grove of old pecan trees that drip with Spanish moss. Materials with the antique patina of age create a realistic portrait of a house from the Creole culture of early-nineteenth-century Louisiana. A weather-beaten picket fence and gate made of haggard old cypress planks borders the sidewalk. Old window shutters with pealing paint and rusted latches hang on the front wall. All of these bits of history come together to create a new, living museum of Creole architecture.

The house is a portrait of another time, made by incorporating artifacts from earlier buildings into its construction. It is seated in a grove of mature trees on the main street where it settles in with older neighbors. Intent on crafting a realistic Creole cottage, Ron used antique materials for windows and doors, lights and latches, mantels and moldings, creating an authentic version of the style with the patina of age. Learning from his restoration projects, the builder fabricated new details patterned after genuine originals so the house would be familiar and convincing.

BUILT FROM ANTIQUE SCRAPS

The house is the sum of old house parts rescued over the years as Ron renovated buildings in the French Quarter of New Orleans. Salvaged French doors and shutters, doorknobs and locksets, flagstones and floorboards were all hand-picked for their age, history,

Here, the classic pavilion roof of French Colonial houses is found under a canopy of gnarled pecan trees, draped with Spanish moss. Separating the property from the street is a rustic picket fence of old cypress planks, called a pieux *fence.*

French Creole houses did not have hallways, so pairs of doors opened directly into two or three front parlors. Five matching sets of salvaged doors and shutters add pieces of history to this facade.

and weathered beauty. With the original patinas carefully preserved through cleaning and storage, these reused antique materials impart a vintage appearance to the house that often fools passers-by.

Ron used his knowledge of buildings in the French Quarter to make decisions about where to incorporate his finds into the house in an authentic way. The trick was to distinguish between materials that were damaged beyond repair and those with only superficial wear and tear and that were durable enough to reuse

Over the years, Ron collected buckets of discarded hardware for doorknobs, locksets, and hinges. When the time came to install five pairs of salvaged French doors, he sorted through his collection for matching parts that were historically correct for an

THE CREOLE PIGEONNIER

→The two-story guest cottage behind the garden's lily pond is designed to look like a traditional Creole *pigeonnier*. Also called a French dovecote or pigeon roost, this plantation structure was typically built beside the main house as an ornamental building designed to house a flock of pigeons, then regarded as a gourmet delicacy. The *pigeonnier* reproduced here is large enough for a kitchen on the first floor and a guest bedroom on the second. Like the main house, the cottage incorporates salvaged weathered French doors, windows, shutters, and other vintage findings.

RECREATING A VERANDA

European sugar planters from the Caribbean islands introduced many characteristics of the French Creole cottage style, such as the veranda, to Louisiana after they arrived in the 1790s. A deep veranda, called a *galerie*, runs across the front of this house. The idea comes from the traditional West Indies cottage, a design adapted to the hot and humid conditions of the tropics. Sheltered beneath the overhang of the hipped roof, the 12-ft.-deep *galerie* affords a cool retreat and a spacious gathering place.

The roof of the cottage is hipped like an elongated pyramid, a French Colonial form known as a pavilion roof, with eaves flared out at the bottom. The eaves are supported by turned wooden

The long galerie porch is a 12-ft.-wide by 40-ft.-long gathering place. The wood-panel ceilings are painted a traditional Creole color called French gros rouge (rust red), and the electric paddle fans are reproductions of early-twentieth-century designs.

This wide door casing is a Greek Revival design from the early nineteenth century.
The door frame appears to hold a set of sliding pocket doors, but it is actually one
antique door cut in half and installed to look like a working pair.

TRADITIONAL CRAFTSMANSHIP
ORIGINAL PAINT COLORS

Each region in early America developed a favored palette of paint colors. French Creoles in Louisiana preferred a rust red, called French *gros rouge*, and a bittersweet green made with arsenic, called Paris green. Other common French Creole colors were Spanish brown, mustard yellow ochre, and butterscotch cream. Painters often mixed their colors on the job site, stirring a paste of white lead into a bucket of linseed oil tinted with mineral powders. Colors were often earth toned and muddy because of the nature of the minerals and dyes used, like iron oxides of red, yellow, and brown, which produced rust reds, yellow ochers, and burnt umbers. Over the years, the linseed oil–based paints yellowed, mellowing the historic hues.

posts, or colonettes (commonly called cigar columns), found on many eighteenth-century French Colonial houses around New Orleans. The upper two thirds of the wooden posts on this new old house are turned in a swelling cylindrical shape, like a classical column, with a capital and base. But the profile of the colonettes is more slender than a classical column, and they belly out in the middle like a cartoon cigar, giving the posts their well-deserved nickname.

NATURE'S AIR-CONDITIONING

The French Creole cottage was inspired by West Indies plantations with raised verandas that were built to capture cooling breezes. Typical of the old West Indies cottages, there are five matched pairs of French doors with shutters in this new house that face the *galerie*. The *galerie* porch opens through these doors directly into twin front parlors, like those that graced the finest nineteenth-century Creole houses, joining indoor and outdoor living spaces. The house has a traditional Creole layout without interior hallways and where one room opens into another, allowing fresh air to circulate freely through the rooms. This simple floor plan idea, which encourages natural air-conditioning, works well in the climate of Louisiana, where the humid environment needs to be considered as part of the design of every house.

The intimate loggia is a porch between two small rooms at the back corners of the Creole cottage, called cabinets. *The exterior walls of secondary spaces in Creole houses were often covered in horizontal shiplapped boards that were smooth but durable. A new crackle-glazed paint finish creates traces of age.*

jambs. The Greek Revival doorway is a historic reference, because the style was the latest fashion when Creole houses flourished (1820–1840). Hanging in each parlor is a cut-glass candelabra on an armature of plated bronze. The antique fixtures look like tiered wedding cakes of glass drops and swags, a style that graced the finest rooms in old Creole houses of the French Quarter.

PAINTED WITH A FRENCH PALETTE

The interiors are painted in a Creole palette of muddy hues that date from the eighteenth century—French *gros rouge* made with iron oxide pigment for the French doors, Paris green made with arsenic pigment for the ceilings, mustard yellow for the window and door trim, and butterscotch cream for the walls. The trim moldings are painted mustard and then ragged with a gray stain to create the discoloration of old and untouched paint.

In the kitchen, the bright Paris green ceilings are made of wood rather than plaster. Wood was the practical ceiling of choice in Creole houses where durable cypress planks were available and where moisture in the air would ruin plaster. Likewise, the walls of the loggia porch, enclosed between the *cabinets*, are sided with flush boards for a smooth, durable covering. The crackle-glaze paint makes the walls look weather scarred, a fitting look for a cottage built of salvaged bits of preserved history.

MARKS OF A CREOLE PARLOR

The builder kept pairs of rescued 8-ft.-tall French doors in his workshop for years, carefully protecting the original crown glass, hardware, paint finish, and wear marks. To complete the set of doors, Ron paired them with traditional exterior shutters, another feature of the West Indies style.

Since Creole cottages do not have a center hall, each of the French doors along the veranda is used as a front door, opening into a parlor. This home's plan is a straightforward adaptation of a typical Creole floor plan but arranged for modern living. The two front parlors are identical, one used as the living room and the other, the dining room.

A large doorway that connects the two parlors is encased in Greek Revival trim with tapered side

Vintage appliances add period character to the new old house, here suggesting a time when the house was updated with a 1940s gas range.

SUNDAY HOUSE
ON THE
PRAIRIE

From a distance, this ranch looks like a mission church—a pure white sculpture framed in a landscape of prairie grass. Homeowner Milton Butcher built this monastic retreat on the Texas prairie east of San Antonio, on land that was once overgrown and neglected. Architect Michael Imber was asked to build a house that recalled the pioneer ranches from the 1840s.

Windows deeply recessed into openings make the walls appear to be the thickness of stone. The 1-ft.-thick walls are constructed of hand-troweled stucco over a wood frame, then painted white to achieve the look of whitewashed Texas German stone houses.

The ranch, in its crisp and severe geometry, is a hybrid of contemporary and traditional forms, which draws inspiration from nineteenth-century Texas German farmhouses and from the spare, taut aesthetic of early modernism. This blending of forms from historic and modern sources *Invents within the Rules* of tradition to make new architecture from old parts. The new ranch is as sturdily built as the old Texas German houses, because it is *Crafted with Natural Materials*, which will endure the test of time. Michael also worked with the landscape of ancient live oaks on the ranch and fit the house into its setting to *Respect the Character of Place*. The house sits in a natural hollow by a pond, under the shelter of a grove of oak trees, a siting tailored to make the new old house look settled in.

HISTORIC PRECEDENT SHAPES THE RANCH

The ranch is inspired by the architecture of Sunday houses, simple weekend retreats built in the German pioneer towns in central Texas during the last half of the nineteenth century. The pattern for the design came from surviving period examples of Sunday houses and early farmhouses in the nearby old German settlements of Castroville and Fredericksburg. The Sunday houses' simple traditional construction

The house sits on a natural fold in the prairie, surrounded by a mature stand of trees so it looks as if it had always been there.

The entry vestibule is an example of Crafting with Natural Materials. *Though French doors were not practical in pioneer houses, they are used here to bring in extra light.*

hallmarks of style
TEXAS GERMAN SUNDAY HOUSE

While Texas was still a sparsely populated Spanish territory in the 1840s, German peasant farmers began to migrate to the frontier. By the time Texas became part of the United States in 1856, small German communities of farms and ranches were spread throughout the Hill Country. A strong heritage of German culture, language, and traditions was imprinted in Texas, including the architecture of simple stone structures, called Sunday houses, made of local limestone rock.

Sunday houses were constructed as places of weekend retreat from the fields, where farmers brought their families for a round of church and socializing. The houses were made of *fachwerk* (timber frame with stone infill) or native limestone coated with stucco and whitewashed inside and out for a clean finish, using building traditions brought from the Old World. The pioneers built austere shelters of one or two rooms under a simple gable roof, with a wooden porch added across the front to keep the houses cool in the parched climate.

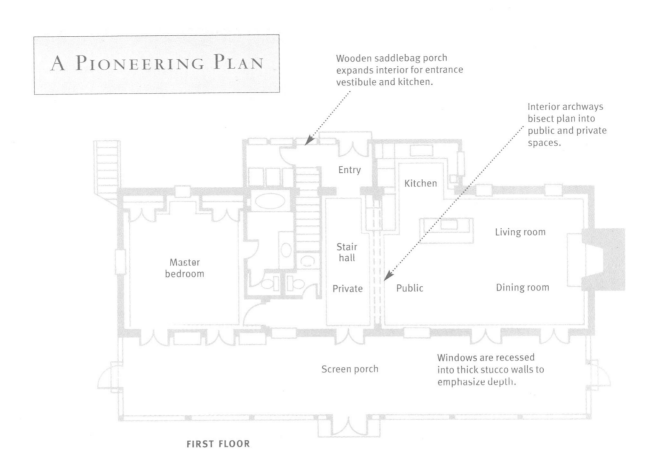

A PIONEERING PLAN

Wooden saddlebag porch expands interior for entrance vestibule and kitchen.

Interior archways bisect plan into public and private spaces.

Entry

Kitchen

Living room

Master bedroom

Stair hall

Private

Public

Dining room

Screen porch

Windows are recessed into thick stucco walls to emphasize depth.

FIRST FLOOR

of limestone rock walls coated with whitewashed plaster, covered by a metal roof, and supporting a wooden porch across the front, became the historic precedent for the ranch.

A TWIST ON TRADITIONAL FEATURES

There are a number of design innovations in this house that create a new take on tradition based on *Inventing within the Rules.* The most striking feature of the house is the bulbous domed chimney breast on the end wall. Its design is a creative fusion of historic forms that Michael saw on old chimneys in early Texas towns, especially the J. P. Tatsch house in Fredericksburg. The new design, plastered in stucco, is a sculptural interpretation of this old-fashioned feature.

A broad plaster arch, thickened to look like a structural stone bearing wall, separates the main living spaces from the bedrooms. The seemingly modern open plan of the main floor, where living, dining, and kitchen areas share a common space, actually mirrors the traditional one-room stube *plan of old German farmhouses.*

Historic references
connect the interior back
to traditional sources.

The hearth is an example of fine craftsmanship. The carved limestone lintel design is patterned after the 100-year-old Mustang grapevine growing next to the house. The slender Roman bricks that are laid in a herringbone pattern inside the firebox are an Old World construction detail.

Rustic wooden porches, colorfully called saddle-bags, were added to the house in honor of the traditional porches that sheltered the original Sunday houses. These saddlebag porches lean against each of the long white exterior walls of the house to expand the interior living space and add outdoor rooms.

HANDCRAFTED EXTERIOR WALLS

The house is meant to look as if it were built of traditional Texas limestone rock. The exterior walls of

the ranch are 12 in. thick and plastered with white stucco, mimicking the stone walls of the Sunday houses (shown on page 172). But the new walls are built of wooden stud framing rather than stone, because authentic limestone construction is labor intensive and costly. The plaster is hand-troweled over the wood frame in an uneven surface of swells and troughs rather than smoothed to perfection. The artistry of the finish is in the handcraftmanship of the undulating texture.

The windows and doors are set back into the wall surface to create deep reveals. These reveals cast strong shadows, just like real stone construction, and reinforce the imagery of walls made of stone. Above the window and door openings, antique mesquite beams are embedded in the plasterwork to form lintels. These weathered lintel beams, wearing a mellow patina of age, were saved from an old barn, weaving fragments of history into the story of the home.

INCORPORATING MODERN INTERIORS

The design of the ranch is a hybrid that shows how modern interiors can be incorporated into a traditional plan without compromising the integrity of a new old house. For example, the house is a long and slender 20-ft. by 64-ft. rectangle that is only one room wide but nearly two stories tall. The narrow width authentically reflects traditional construction, because the short length of native oak timbers

The living room has a mission church quality—a sanctuary with soaring ceilings, a fireplace as altar, and clerestory windows that cast beams of light. The ceiling conceals ductwork, a way of Incorporating Modern Conveniences *within the structure.*

TRADITIONAL CRAFTSMANSHIP
WOODEN PLANK PARTITION WALLS

Before the introduction of gypsum wallboard, interior partitions in early farmhouses were traditionally made of boards attached together to form a wall. While plaster applied over split wood lath was common for mid-nineteenth-century city houses, the technique was labor intensive and time-consuming for a prudent Texas German farmer, who simply wanted to divide up the interior of his house.

A simple partition could be made with thin, wide boards joined together and installed from floor to ceiling without any structural frame. Planks were normally 1 in. thick and varied randomly in width from 6 in. to 18 in., depending on the available wood. The edges were interlocked with a continuous tongue-and-groove joint, often decorated with a running bead where the boards meet. Although thin and inexpensive to build, these wooden partitions were sturdy and long-lasting, the perfect solution for a thrifty German pioneer.

The horizontal lapped siding that frames the staircase is painted in sagebrush green and recalls the traditional plank wall partitions of German farmhouses.

available for roof beams limited the width of early Texas houses.

The 20-ft.-high cathedral ceiling of the living room is framed with longleaf pine rafter beams and ceiling planks, a material that substitutes for traditional oak beams. The raised plaster chimneypiece at the far end of the room has an altar-like presence, with a carved limestone panel above the fireplace that recalls an Old World construction detail.

Three walls of the living room are painted pure white, the surfaces barely interrupted by small clerestory windows placed high above eye level. These small openings are called gunport windows because they were originally used for defense against American Indian attacks. The pristine white walls below the windows are a gallery for the homeowner's collection of twentieth-century art, a design consideration that explains the spare modern look of the interior.

The homeowner, a photographer and an art collector, wanted modern spatial clarity within the otherwise traditional house. While the open interior plan reflects the traditional *stube* parlor of a Texas German farmhouse, the vaulted space is also a modern gallery loft. The lines are clean and simple with trim moldings, baseboards, and decorative surfaces paired down to be minimal

TRACES OF FARMHOUSE DETAILS

Beyond the modern lines, there are clear connections back to the farmhouse tradition, from the wrought-iron wagon wheel chandeliers, to the floors of red-brown Oklahoma flagstone, which imitate the packed-dirt floors of early German farmhouses.

The theme of thick stone walls appears again in the interior, where arches seem to be cut through deep stonework. At the midpoint in the length of the house, a tall archway bisects the floor plan, like an interior bearing wall of stone masonry. The main staircase climbs between two wooden plank walls that run across the width of the house. These walls are made of 1-in.-thick tongue-and-groove panels that resemble wooden farmhouse partition walls. These historic references connect the interior back to traditional sources.

A series of smaller arches cuts through the plaster wall along the front of the house, connecting the interior space to the wooden saddlebag porch addition leaning against the front facade. One of these niches carved through the wall holds the kitchen, designed with simple Shaker-style cabinets and unadorned wooden plank countertops. Another arch links the stair hall to the entry vestibule, and a third arch is the passageway for the staircase to the second-floor bedroom.

The wooden partition walls and door trims are painted in earth tones of sagebrush green and rust

The kitchen blends contemporary materials, such as the stainless-steel range hood and wall of white glazed commercial tile, with simple farmhouse design elements, in the form of plain Shaker cabinets and counters made of solid Spanish cedar. Red-brown flagstone underfoot creates the illusion of an old farmhouse dirt floor.

The transom window in the front hall looks as if it could be a remnant from when the front door was relocated to the front porch. This ghost from times past reflects what often happened as old houses were added onto, an example of how to weave bits of historical realism into a new old house.

The porch of this new old house functions much as it did for traditional pioneer living.

red, which are reproductions of historic San Antonio colors. Floors are paved with large irregular slabs of red-brown Oklahoma sandstone that match the color of the soils around the ranch. These soils were once used to make the packed-dirt floors of nineteenth-century Texas farmhouses.

THE SADDLEBAG PORCH

Through pairs of French doors, the living room and master bedroom open onto a screen porch, another saddlebag, that runs the full length of the back wall of the house. The deep reveals cut into the wall around the windows and doors show how the thick paste of stucco has been worked into an imperfect undulating surface for a hand-tooled look. The edges of the stucco are rounded over at the corners to form soft contours, called pillowed edges. Together, the rippling wall surface and pillowed corners enhance the illusion of stucco over stone.

The porch of this new old house functions much as it did for traditional pioneer living, when sheltering porches provided the only relief from the Texas sun and heat. By day, the porch is an outdoor living and dining room, and by night it becomes a sleeping porch with Murphy beds mounted inside cabinets attached to the wall. The screen porch is positioned on the southeast side to capture the prevailing breezes, respecting an orientation favored by the early German settlers as a method of naturally cooling their houses.

The open framework of the porch appears to lean against sturdy masonry walls, earning it the name lean-to. *The floors are irregular slabs of Oklahoma flagstone, the color of the native red Texas soil, meant to simulate the hard dirt floors of early farmhouses.*

A PORTRAIT
OF
LOUISIANA
HERITAGE

Architect Ken Tate has drawn together themes from Louisiana's heritage for a new old French Colonial house in Mississippi. The house borrows from the traditions of the River Road plantations, the Creole townhouses of the French Quarter, and the Acadian cottages of bayou country.

The roof eaves of this French Colonial plantation house are flared in a bell-cast curve. Reclaimed antique roof slates and clay ridge tiles from New Orleans show the weathered surface that conveys The Patina of Age.

Ken learned to mix these strains from the master of Louisiana vernacular, architect Hays Town, whose twentieth-century revival of French Colonial style pioneered the use of antique materials and traditional craftsmanship to recreate historic details in new houses. This new old house, built of several parts, looks as if it had grown by successive additions, each part drawn from a distinct type of eighteenth-century French Colonial architecture: plantation, townhouse, and cottage.

The house is new and yet has a veneer of age that makes it appear mature, settled, and venerable. Layers of antique building materials for slate roofs, brick walls, and heart pine floors *Create the Patina of Age*. Combined with *Details for Authenticity* in the plaster columns, a pavilion roof, and shuttered French doors, these features convey the hallmarks of the French tradition. This palette of historic motifs is appropriately placed, correctly proportioned, and carefully constructed in the old-fashioned way to recreate a genuine portrait of historic style.

A VILLAGE OF BUILDINGS

Ken faced the problem of translating a historic style based on small vernacular houses into a house of larger scale. Rather than inflate the size of the original French Colonial precedents, he decided to divide the building plan into smaller parts. Each part of the plan—the formal rooms, the bedrooms, and the garage—is a discrete building with its own clearly defined character. By inventing a new arrangement within the rules of style, Ken disguised the size of the house in a collection of five buildings and humbled the ambitious floor plan to preserve the comfortable proportions of a period home.

On first approach, the house appears to be a long and low plantation house encircled by a row of columns that carry an imposing hipped roof, punctuated by slender spindles for chimneys. The

A colonnade on the garden facade carries the roof over the galerie *porch. The patio, bordered by brick planter boxes, is paved with flagstones and handmade bricks laid in a basketweave pattern, which suggests a French Quarter courtyard garden.*

hallmarks of style
FRENCH COLONIAL PLANTATION

he eighteenth-century French, Spanish, and West Indies settlers of the Louisiana territory developed a Creole architectural style of mixed heritage adapted to the sultry heat of the Mississippi Delta. The early Creole house was a simple plan of two or three rooms in a row, with *galerie* porches across the front and back. Sheltered under a French hipped roof supported by a colonnade of posts, the house was raised above the ground on piers.

The traditional Creole house became more sophisticated on the large sugar plantations found along the banks of the Mississippi. On the historic plantations, many smaller structures were concentrated around the principal house, including a freestanding kitchen, a plantation office, a privy, and a pair of *pigeon-niers* (pigeon roosts). The varied structures were often knit together by landscape walls and formal gardens. The architect borrowed the inspiration from this village of buildings for the layout of this new old house.

Inspired by eighteenth-century Creole townhouses the two-story bedroom wing shows Spanish influences that are reproduced in the gable-end walls with raised parapets, cantilevered second-floor balcony, and projecting bay window (called a reja*).*

columns that initially seem diminutive are almost 12 ft. tall and nearly 2 ft. in diameter. The two chimneys that seem impossibly slender from afar are spires that tower 25 ft. in the air.

The house is a village of buildings that are subtly interconnected, recalling the complex arrangement of a plantation house and its outbuildings on the sugar plantations along Louisiana's River Road. At the center is a classic French Colonial plantation house of the mid-eighteenth century, covered by a broad hipped, or pavilion, roof. Inside are the formal rooms of the house as well as the kitchen and sitting room. Surrounding this central plantation house is a staggered, tight-knit cluster of smaller buildings.

On one side is a two-story master bedroom suite styled like the Creole townhouses of the French Quarter. On the other side, a floor-to-ceiling arched studio window centers on the facade of a

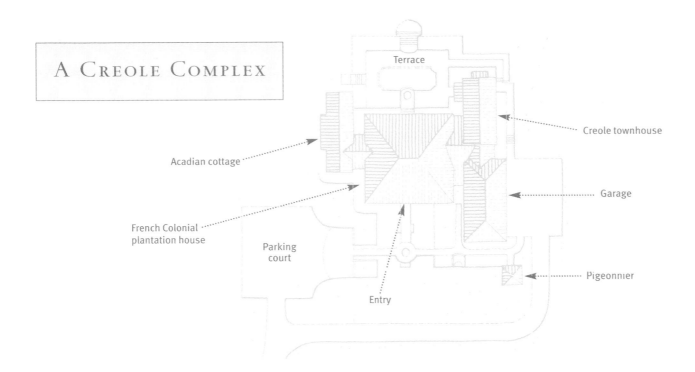

Terrace

Creole townhouse

Acadian cottage

Garage

French Colonial plantation house

Parking court

Pigeonnier

Entry

one-story Acadian brick cottage, where the children's bedrooms reside. These visually distinct parts are all linked together by recessed connections.

AUTHENTIC MATERIALS

The house is rendered authentic by vintage materials and methods of construction. Many eighteenth-century plantation houses were surrounded by *galerie* porches under an umbrella-shaped pavilion roof, held aloft by classical columns. In the new old house, the *galerie* porch is formed by a colonnade of Tuscan columns. The authentic techniques used to model the exteriors of the house reflect Ken's study of French Colonial methods. For instance, the Tuscan columns could have been made of wood or cast in gypsum, but French Colonial plantation columns were traditionally made of brick plastered with stucco. The architect insisted that the construction be historically correct, even though the concealed brickwork would not show.

The gnarled texture of walls laid in clinker bricks is visible on the wall of the family entrance hall. Infill walls of horizontal shiplap siding finish the end of the room, with a decorative ocular window.

The space linking the kitchen to the master bedroom wing is the family entrance hall. The long, narrow room, sandwiched between lime washed rough brick walls, is meant to look like an infill space that has been renovated. Walls of horizontal shiplap siding avoid drywall.

For the roof structure, the wooden rafters project out beyond the column line to support eaves that overhang the house by several feet. The ends of these rafters, called the rafter tails, are shaped in a scalloped pattern, which is a traditional French Colonial decorative detail. The top surface of the shaped rafter tails rise in a curve that lifts the skirt of the roof in a flared edge, called a bell-cast eaves.

The *galerie* porches under the roof are also constructed in the French Colonial tradition. Stout wooden timbers span between columns to bear the weight of the roof framing and ceiling beams. A web of heavy beams and smaller purlins, or cross beams, tie the columns to the wall and support wooden planks that form the finished ceiling. The ceiling beams are painted cypress timbers, which are the traditional construction material for roofs because of the wood's natural ability to resist rot.

Details for the raised parapets and cantilevered balcony on the two-story bedroom wing reveal the influence of Spanish building traditions on French Colonial architecture, during the time Spain ruled Louisiana (1763–1801). The walls are roughly surfaced with irregular bricks called clinkers—the reject bricks pulled from the discard pile at the brickyard. The masons laid the brick walls unevenly, leaving unpointed mortar between bricks for a rough-cast texture. Coated with layers of quick lime, a type of whitewash applied thinly, the brickwork takes on a rich mottled surface character that looks old.

The front entrance hall is a feature adapted from formal French architecture. Traditional French Colonial plantation houses opened directly into a salon and did not have an enclosed entry hall.

The painted walls of the entrance hall are finished with vertical boards trimmed by panel moldings. A ⅛-in. gap separates each board to make it stand out. Highlighted in buttercream paint, the room has a French country decor that updates the French Colonial plantation with later renovations.

In plantation house tradition, French doors of antique cypress open into the living room from the galerie porches to bring light and air into the room. The exposed grid of heavy beams and purlins that form the ceiling are finished with beaded edges and painted sage green in the fashion of eighteenth-century woodwork.

The fictional history of its creation
makes the house appear timeless
and mature in its setting.

AN UNCONVENTIONAL PLANTATION PLAN

Ken responded to the homeowner's need for a house that lives primarily on one level by dividing the plan into three parts: the main house, which serves as living room, dining room, and kitchen; and two separate sections for private bedroom wings. This tripartite plan (floor plan not shown) has no real precedent in the French Colonial tradition. Instead, Ken devised a unique suite of rooms that are informally arranged in an almost quirky plan. His free adaptation of the interior layout for this traditional plantation house *Invents within the Rules*, creating a plan that works for modern living.

There is no hallway that runs through the center of the house to organize rooms on either side. Instead, the main rooms fan out from an entry vestibule, which leads directly into a corner of the living room. From there, the living room, dining room, and kitchen open into one another, often off axis, with each room having its own distinctive character. Pairs of French doors with arched transoms join the formal rooms to the outdoor *galeries.*

The entry vestibule is a hybrid of vernacular finishes and classical details that give this new room, inserted in a plantation house plan, an elegant French country character (shown on pages 190 and 191). The walls are paneled in vertical wooden boards that recall the plank walls used for partitions in early eighteenth-century French Colonial houses.

Authentic details include a French country raised hearth and antique New Orleans brick floors. The hearth is sculpted in plaster and topped with a tapered chimney hood. The herringbone patterned floors are finished with oil, wax, and coffee grounds.

Unlike the historic original construction method, the paneling boards are perfectly spaced and uniform in width for a well-ordered appearance.

Classical panel moldings overlay the walls in a stylized pattern of picture frames, which resemble the urbane interiors of French New Orleans townhouses. Floors made of vintage New Orleans tan bricks are laid in a herringbone pattern between diagonal ribs of old heart pine, and finished with an unusual recipe of tung oil, carnauba wax, and coffee grounds to achieve a soft patina.

AN ACCIDENTAL SPACE

As so often happens in planning a house, the undefined, leftover spaces between planned rooms become uniquely rich and lively. One such space is the connecting link between the kitchen and the master bedroom wing, where the family entrance, mudroom, and garage all intersect in a hallway (shown on page 190). The long, narrow room is sandwiched between lime washed brick walls that look like old exterior walls. Almost haphazard in its mix of materials, the room is tailored to look like a renovation from successive eras of construction, a clever fabrication that Ken pulled together to tell a story of changes over time.

TRADITIONAL CRAFTSMANSHIP
CLINKERS AND SALVAGED BRICKS

↣ The lime washed brick walls of the two bedroom wings are made of bricks called clinkers. These are rejects from the brick kiln, which have been over-burned, blackened, or even twisted in the process of firing the bricks. Normally discarded for their imperfections, the clinkers are structurally sound, and the architect chose to use them to build the heavily textured walls.

The bricks are laid in ragged layers, and the excess mortar between them is scraped off unevenly, rather than tightly packed, to exaggerate the irregularities. The noticeably sloppy workmanship of the bricklaying is intentional, because the mottled texture gives the walls an untutored, handmade appearance, which simulates old brickwork.

The *pigeonnier*, garden walls, and chimneys are constructed with old bricks salvaged from demolished buildings in New Orleans. These bricks, recovered from leveled antique buildings, convincingly *Create the Patina of Age*. Called New Orleans reds, the wall bricks on the *pigeonnier* have a salmon-rust color range.

The pigeonnier, *a French dovecote or pigeon roost, serves as a garden shed. Made of antique bricks and roof slates, it is a classic outbuilding unique to French Colonial plantations. The* pigeonnier *was often paired with a* garconniere, *or young boys' quarters, arranged around the main house.*

The galerie is a comfortable Southern veranda outfitted with paddle fans and reproduction nineteenth-century gas lanterns. The 11-ft. 6-in.-tall Tuscan columns tower above the flagstone floor, like the robust columns that encircled the ground floor of historic plantation houses.

HOUSE
OF FINE
WOODWORKING

The bungalow that architect Curtis Gelotte designed for homeowners in the Seattle area could have fallen right out of the pages of *The Craftsman* magazine, published by furniture designer Gustav Stickley from 1901 to 1916 to promote the Arts and Crafts movement in America. The style celebrates the nobility of craftsmanship.

Early Craftsman designs offered simple, practical open floor plans that promoted the flow of light and air through the house. A low wall of wooden paneling forms the traditional screen used between rooms in Craftsman interiors.

purred on by clients passionate about the Arts and Crafts style, Curt married the discipline of fine craftsmanship with Stickley's forward-looking planning theories to create a classic bungalow. Like the house plans that Stickley offered to readers in his journal, the new old bungalow nestles into the landscape dressed in natural wooden shingles and earth-tone colors. Crafted in wood and stone, the construction details are clearly expressed to make it simple to read the way the house is built. The floor plan is arranged in a compact flow of rooms that are artistically conceived and yet make effective use of space. Curt's design is an authentic essay in the elemental simplicity and no-nonsense attitude of Craftsman bungalow architecture.

Quarried granite blocks on the entrance piers and stone foundations tie the bungalow to the landscape. Reproduction Arts and Crafts copper light fixtures are plentiful today.

REVERENCE FOR CRAFTSMANSHIP

The bungalow is pressed into a hillside site overlooking Lake Washington, a Seattle neighborhood where the preservation of lake views is critical. With its first floor set 4 ft. below grade, the horizontal figure of the house seems to fit snug to the ground, a natural repose encouraged in the Craftsman tradition.

Craftsman architecture celebrates the use of indigenous natural materials, such as wood and stone, that tie the house to the landscape around it. Curt used stone retaining walls and banked gardens to hold back the earth across the narrow width of the property. The clapboard and shingle walls of the one-and-a-half story house sit on a stone foundation

made of rough granite blocks, a way to make the house look as if it were built on a rock outcrop.

The reverence for craftsmanship of the Arts and Crafts period expressed itself in bungalows in which the details of construction were made visible. Especially on porches and deep overhanging roof eaves, the carpenters' woodworking details were exaggerated as a form of simple ornamentation. In the new old bungalow, the eaves are supported by decorative tri-

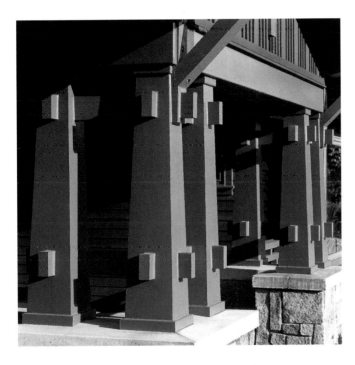

The square porch columns are arranged more for artistic effect than for structural necessity. Clustered at the corners in groups of three, the short, stout posts are battered, or tapered outward, in a classic Arts and Crafts form and tied together with decorative horizontal timbers.

The bungalow has a low, spreading profile accentuated by shallow roofs with long overhanging eaves and windows arranged in horizontal bands.

hallmarks of style
THE CRAFTSMAN BUNGALOW

urniture designer Gustav Stickley and his colleagues in the American Arts and Crafts movement conceived of a new type of home that was suited for everybody— a practical and well-crafted alternative to the overwrought villas of the late nineteenth century. Craftsman homes were economical to build, yet they were finished with the best natural materials and finest fittings. They were designed to showcase the craftsmanship of artisans returning to the traditional handicrafts of masonry, woodworking, weaving, metal-smithing, ceramics, and glass.

Through *The Craftsman*, Stickley offered free plans for bungalow houses, which become known as the Craftsman style.

The idea for the Craftsman bungalow was originally adopted from India, where British colonial officers were housed in simple, one-story cottages with deep verandas. Practical bungalow homes, appealing for their utility and simplicity of construction, were eventually sold as precut kits through the Sears, Roebuck catalog and transported by railroad across the United States to become the first mass-market house style.

angular brackets, and the roof rafters have shaped ends cut with a scrollsaw, which reveal the craft of building.

The elaborate construction of the front porch ties this house to traditional bungalow character. Designed to convey a Craftsman signature, the porch has its own sheltering roof supported by an intricate framework of columns. The columns are clustered in groups of three short, square posts that taper toward the base, a flared shape that is a classic Craftsman feature. Where the posts are tied together by horizontal timbers, their carpentry joints are exaggerated for artistic effect. The square columns provide a vertical accent against the horizontal lines of the house

Each floor of the facade is finished with its own natural material—from stone to clapboard to shingles—to highlight the layering of textures and to reinforce the horizontal lines of the house. The

The front door is recessed under the covered porch, framed within walls of redwood clapboard siding. Colors used on the woodwork, like the khaki green posts and the caramel clapboards, are muted earth tones, favored in Arts and Crafts work because they imitate nature.

AN OPEN FLOOR PLAN

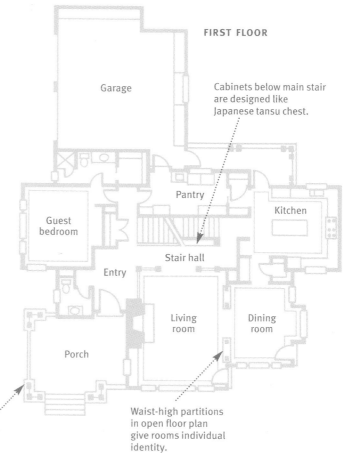

FIRST FLOOR

Garage

Cabinets below main stair are designed like Japanese tansu chest.

Pantry

Kitchen

Guest bedroom

Stair hall

Entry

Living room

Dining room

Porch

Tapered porch posts are distinctive Arts and Crafts feature.

Waist-high partitions in open floor plan give rooms individual identity.

The dining room is criss-crossed by Douglas fir ceiling beams and trim details that balance rich dark woodwork against cream white walls. A plate rail for the display of art treasures rings the walls, a feature borrowed from medieval English interiors for Arts and Crafts homes.

The floor plan flows freely among the living room, dining room, and entrance hall, separated by half walls designed as display cabinets. The wood-paneled tray ceiling is a unique design innovation for a Craftsman home, and the hammered copper light fixtures with flower-bud glass shades show the reverence for nature in the style.

foundations are made of rough blocks of Puget Sound granite and their weathered faces are exposed, as is the chimney of tapered stone that pokes through the roof. On the main floor, northwest redwood clapboards are stained the color of caramel, while the second-floor gable ends and pair of squat dormers are finished in bark brown shingles.

COLORS OF NATURE

Part of the Craftsman philosophy was that of getting back to nature, and this spirit is captured in natural materials and color tones. The new bungalow is painted in a palette of dark earth-tone stains, a traditional color scheme that expresses the reverence for nature in the Craftsman style.

Details of the Douglas fir mantelpiece include colorful handmade art tiles incised with natural patterns. The tiles exemplify the Arts and Crafts worship of the art of making utilitarian objects beautiful.

Craftsman architecture celebrates the use of indigenous natural materials that tie the house to the landscape around it.

Curt describes his color scheme for the house as having "muted greens and muted browns with splashes of colors that come from garden flowers." The exterior siding is stained in muddy tones of caramel and bark. The architect used semitransparent stains with a small amount of pigment in the mix to reveal the grain of the wood. Paint is used to highlight the woodworking details. The tapered porch posts, rafter tails, and roof brackets, which support the overhangs, are picked out in a khaki green color. Contrasting with the earthen shades of the walls, the window sashes are stained a poppy red to accent the frames against the dark walls.

A STAGE FOR THE CARPENTER'S CRAFT

The artistry of the carpenters is displayed in interior woodwork details crafted of Douglas fir, done with a furnituremaker's care for precise joinery. The formal rooms are covered in the warm amber tones of wood paneling, ceiling beams, and trim moldings. At the heart of the floor plan, a broad staircase fills the entrance hall, handcrafted with a handrail of interlaced horizontal and vertical spindles ending in a stout newel post. The fretwork balustrade recalls the details of a staircase in a 1907 San Francisco Arts and Crafts home.

The cabinetwork under the stair treads is a reference to Asian influences in Arts and Crafts design—in particular, the artistic Japanese wood-

OPENING THE FLOW OF ROOMS

"The house is an old-fashioned plan of isolated rooms coupled with a modern open plan," says the architect. The living room, dining room, and entry vestibule fan out around the staircase. Each room has a distinctive identity, but all appear to flow together because the walls between rooms are low. Waist-high partitions like these were the traditional way to separate rooms, developed for the Craftsman style at the turn of the twentieth century. This modern open spatial flow reflects the new attitude toward room planning championed in Craftsman design, which encouraged the healthful flow of light and air between rooms.

BRINGING DAYLIGHT INSIDE

In the frequently overcast conditions of the Pacific Northwest, bringing daylight into a house wherever possible is paramount. Knowing that the stained woodwork would make the rooms dark and that the period light fixtures with low-wattage bulbs would not provide much light, Curt designed a decorative glass skylight over the main staircase.

Searching for other ways to brighten the interiors, the architect wired the house for programmed lighting, incorporating modern technology to enhance tradition. This authentic Craftsman bungalow is an innovative variation on the modern tradition of the handmade house that fuses exquisite carpentry with advances in technology and a flowing floor plan.

working style that captured the imagination of the movement's leading architects, Greene and Greene, in their early-twentieth-century Pasadena houses.

Curt incorporated a woodworking innovation in the design of the living room ceiling, carving a cove or tray out of the open attic above the room to add a cathedral effect. The tray ceiling is paneled in Douglas fir, with crown molding around the perimeter to conceal recessed lights. A simple detail that adds character to the room, the cathedral ceiling seems perfectly at home in the Arts and Crafts interior, although it is an unusual variation seldom seen in the originals.

A skylight of colored glass illuminates the stair hall. A glass artist sprinkled colored chips across the surface of a translucent sheet and fused them together to create strokes of melted green and red glass.

NEW ENGLAND
IN THE
NORTHWEST

Patrice and Kevin Auld built a new house in the Pacific Northwest, designed to reproduce the distinctive architecture of the Shingle Style developed in New England during the late nineteenth century. Because areas of the Northwest coast are reminiscent of Maine, they thought the Shingle Style would fit in well on the boulder-strewn, fir-laden shores of Puget Sound.

The lively contrast between ivory-painted trim on windows and moldings and the dark texture of shingles is a trademark of Shingle Style houses. Shingles molded around curved jambs to reach recessed windows exaggerate the soft, round form and thickness of the wall.

The house shows how it is possible to bring a regional traditional style to another part of the country by understanding how the features work together and by finding a landscape setting where it will look best. The style, created by architects of the time and made popular from 1880 to 1910, was inspired by old colonial houses in New England villages that were made of weathered shingles with white trim. This Shingle Style house here in the Northwest honors several of the Pillars of Traditional Design. Together, they make this house stand out as a perfect example of how a new old house can be achieved.

First, the homeowners and their architect, Stuart Silk, studied the character of the chosen site. Then,

The house carves a long and rambling silhouette along the shore of Puget Sound. The composition of the house is also influenced by the symmetry of the Colonial Revival, with its prominent center gable, pair of shed dormers, and companion porches.

Symmetry is appealing in a new old house, because we are instinctually drawn to things in balanced pairs.

by bringing together classic elements of the Shingle Style in a new design, they explored the creative potential of *Inventing within the Rules* of traditional style. Last, exterior walls covered in uniform rows of cedar shingles and accented by three sturdy stone chimneys, celebrate the beauty of *Crafting with Natural Materials*, which will age gracefully and are *Built for the Ages.*

COLONIAL SYMMETRY IN THE SHINGLE STYLE

The Shingle Style elements of this new old house are composed in a fresh way and not copied directly from an older house, showing how one architect worked creatively with the language of a tradition— and *Invented within the Rules.*

The gambrel roof is a signature feature of the house, a double-pitched shape that is familiar from eighteenth-century Dutch Colonial style houses. Favored by Shingle Style architects, the gambrel has twin slopes with a shallow incline at the peak and steeply pitched sides. A Dutch gable frames the front entrance to the house, supporting a balcony under its draping eaves, which sits on stout brackets above the front door. Details of the balcony and gable are Georgian, such as the paneled posts, the balustrade, and the elaborate cornice.

On the waterside facade of the house, Stuart worked the theme of symmetry into the composition. Symmetry is appealing in a new old house,

because we are drawn to things in balanced pairs, an instinct that begins with our reading of the human body. So when we see a house in balance, intuition tells us that it has familiar features, even though it may have odd quirks.

Another Dutch gable centers the waterside facade of the house, perfectly framed by twin stone chimneys and by a pair of shed dormers, which are symmetrical. A pair of porches glassed-in with French doors, flank the gable, one for the sun porch and the other for the breakfast room, suggesting symmetry. But the porches are of different shapes— one a square bay and the other an octagonal bay— balanced, but not identical.

SEEING SHINGLES WITH FRESH EYES

Stuart explored the flexible, artistic qualities of shingles for the decorative treatment of the facades, just as the original Shingle Style architects had discovered their expressive possibilities. *Crafting with Natural Materials*, the architect used this new old house as a blank canvas for inventive details. In the upper trian-

The Dutch front door, painted a classic colonial dark green black, sits in a frame of multipaned sidelights and transom windows. A view straight through the house from the front door is used to draw the eye across the floor plan to a distant vista or landscape feature.

DISTRESSED FLOORS

➤ Flooring is the most prominent finish material that has the ability to make a new house look authentic and old. If you don't want to use old boards but want the look of antiqued wood, distressing, a technique used on new wood, will *Create the Patina of Age.*

In this house, new hickory-pecan floorboards are handworked on a bench before the floor is laid. Using a hand scraper with a curved blade, the craftsmen carve an irregular pattern of shallow channels into the board, creating a rippled surface. Then the floorboards are installed in the traditional manner. With the floors in place, the finishers return to scrape the joints between adjoining boards so that the channels blend from one board to the next. Then they apply a mixture of walnut- and mahogany-colored dyes to stain the floor an antique cordovan color. Followed by several coats of tung oil to deepen the finish, the floors are buffed out with a steel-wool pad and finished with satin-sheen polyurethane.

Interior finishing techniques soften and age this new Shingle Style house to make it look like it's been lived in for many generations.

The walnut-stained floorboards, made of 10-in.- to 12-in.-wide boards of hickory-pecan, are furrowed with a curved scraper for a handplaned look.

gle of the Dutch gable, the wall shingles sweep outward in a gracious curve over a horizontal molding, called a belt course, which prolongs the horizontal line of the roof. Grouped in pairs, the second-story windows are set into deep recesses that accentuate the depth of the wall, using shingles that are rolled around cylindrical jambs. And the base of the wall terminates in a flared skirt that girdles the perimeter of the house.

The treatment for the open porch at the end of the house is even more whimsical; here, the shingles play artful games on the facade. The porch is burrowed into the body of the house through cavelike openings in the wall. Shingles crest over the curved arches in compressed waves and cascade down the piers toward rock foundations. These playful artistic effects delighted early architects of the style, who patterned shingles in wavy lines, cut them into fancy shapes, and coaxed them into rustic textures.

A Summerhouse Plan

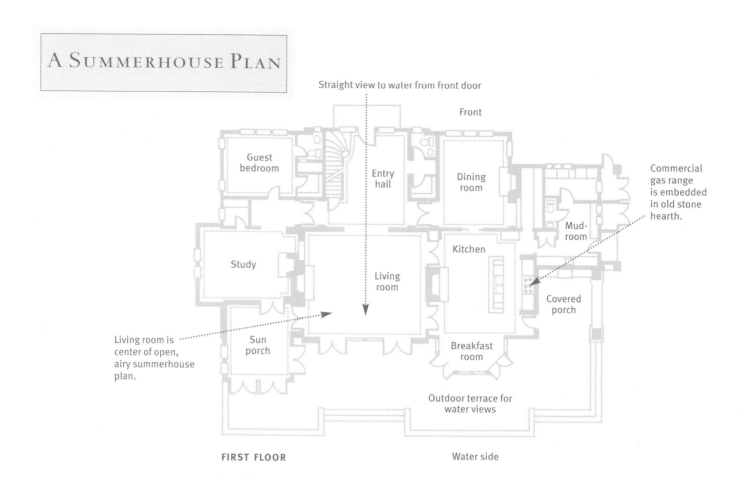

Straight view to water from front door

Front

Guest bedroom

Entry hall

Dining room

Commercial gas range is embedded in old stone hearth.

Mud-room

Study

Kitchen

Covered porch

Living room

Living room is center of open, airy summerhouse plan.

Sun porch

Breakfast room

Outdoor terrace for water views

FIRST FLOOR

Water side

SUMMERHOUSE INTERIORS

On a clear day, you can look straight through the Auld house to a breathtaking view of Puget Sound, with Mount Rainier in the background. The view begins at the front door and passes through the living room to a wall of French doors on the waterside. At the top of the homeowners' wish list, the through view was the major requirement for the design, and it organizes the floor plan. The architect planned the vista down a center hall and then arranged the kitchen, living room, and sun porch in a perpendicular line along the water, making a T-shape plan. With this plan, all the main living spaces have water views through a wall of windows overlooking the sound.

The front entrance to the house is a Dutch door made of upper and lower panels that are separately hinged but can be locked together to open as one. Although not strictly authentic for a colonial revival Shingle Style house, which was more likely to have had a raised-panel entrance door, the Dutch door may allude to the Dutch gambrel shape of the roof and offers another way to capture the view.

SOFTENING THE INTERIORS

The many interior finishing techniques that Stuart explored to make this new house look old—from checked wall panels using green lumber to distressed floors using hand tools—soften and age this Shingle Style house to make it believable. And his scripted

The kitchen is a showpiece of rustic lodge character. A fieldstone wall spanned by a hewn mantel-tree beam resembles a New England colonial keeping-room hearth, filled in with cabinets and a hammered-copper beehive dome hood. Unlacquered brass gooseneck faucets and a ceramic farm sink mounted under a wooden plank countertop add vintage character.

The fireplace, crafted of native quarried granite ledgestone, speaks of the renewed interest in stonemasonry for new old houses.

A child's bedroom has the atmosphere of a cozy cottage. The unlacquered cast brass hinges, slide bolts, and handles on the French doors are a special-order finish that naturally tarnishes, giving the hardware a mellow, hand-rubbed patina over time.

stories of changes over time make the house look lived in for generations.

The hardwood floors are striking because they looks antique—and perfectly preserved. Though the wood is new, the wide hickory-pecan boards were tooled and stained in a rustic finish that duplicates the look of old handplaned floors. The finish is an astonishing example of *Creating the Patina of Age,* done by hand one board at a time. It is a painstaking finishing technique, which was used in every room of the house.

At the heart of the house, the living room is furnished with sun-bleached fabrics, quilts, and hooked rugs, which reproduce the comfortably laid-back decor of an old seaside summerhouse, as many of the early Shingle Style houses have become. There is no drywall in the living room—or anywhere in the

house, for that matter. Instead, all of the walls and ceilings are finished with random-width boards and wooden paneling. The boards are installed partially green, which means they are not completely dried. They split and crack (or check) as they dry out, to look like old wooden paneling weathered by time. Then every inch of woodwork is painted a cream white for a mellow, airy beach house look. With such fine materials used throughout the house, this is certainly a home *Built for the Ages.*

A NEW OLD COLONIAL KITCHEN

The summerhouse theme changes in the kitchen, where the materials are more hardy and rustic, like an old cabin or lodge. The idea here was to suggest an early colonial kitchen—complete with antique barn beams that frame the ceiling and a countertop made of thick pine planks, which look rescued from colonial times—that tells a story of many changes over time. All of the finishes are purposely staged to recount a fictitious story of renovations to an older kitchen, while preserving apparent vestiges of history.

The light-soaked living room has painted timber ceiling beams with checked faces that look aged. Shingled walls painted mint green in the adjoining sun porch suggest that the porch was once open to the outdoors, Telling a Story Over Time.

Ron Arnoult
Arnoult Renovations
P. O. Box 185
Madisonville, LA 70447
(985) 845-8887

Michael Bauer
Bauer, Freeman, McDermott
Architects
1424 Paseo De Peralta
Santa Fe, NM 87501
(505) 988-1905
www.bfmarc.com

Thomas Bollay
Thomas Bollay Associates
P. O. Box 5686
Montecito, CA 93150
(805) 969-1991
www.architect.com

Donald Cooper
Cooper Johnson Smith
Architects, Inc.
102 South 12th St.
Tampa, FL 33602
(813) 273-0034
www.cjsarch.com

William Curtis
and Russell Windham
Curtis & Windham Architects
3815 Montrose Boulevard, Suite 100
Houston, TX 77006
(713) 942-7251

Curtis Gelotte
Curtis Gelotte Architects
150 Lake St. South, Suite 208
Kirkland, WA 98033
(425) 828-3081
www.gelotte.com

Outerbridge Horsey
and Merle Thorpe, *practicing as*:
Outerbridge Horsey Associates
1228 ½ 31st St. NW
Washington, DC 20007
(202) 337-4826
and
MTGB Architects
1025 Connecticut Ave., NW,
Suite 1000
Washington, DC 20036
(202) 298-7771

Michael Imber
Michael G. Imber Architect
111 West El Prado
San Antonio, TX 78212
(210) 824-7703
www.michaelgimber.com

Marc Rueter
Rueter Associates Architects
515 5th St.
Ann Arbor, MI 48103
(734) 769-0070

Gil Schafer III
G. P. Schafer Architect, PLLC
225 Lafayette St., Room 804
New York, NY 10012
(917) 237-1552

Gregory Schipa
The Weather Hill Company, Ltd.
P. O. Box 113
Charlotte, VT 05445
(802) 425-2095
www.weatherhillcompany.com

Stuart Silk
Stuart Silk Architects
2400 North 45th St.
Seattle, WA 98103
(206) 728-9500
www.stuartsilk.com

Jim Strickland
Historical Concepts, Inc.
430 Prime Point, Suite 103
Peachtree City, GA 30269
(770) 487-8041
www.historicalconcepts.com

Ken Tate
Ken Tate Architect
206 Covington St.
Madisonville, LA 70447
(985) 845-8181
www.kentatearchitect.com

Russell Versaci
Versaci Neumann & Partners
Architects
205 East Washington St.
Middleburg, VA 20117
(540) 687-3917
www.versacineumann.com

Peter Zimmerman
Peter Zimmerman Architects
828 Old Lancaster Rd.
Berwyn, PA 19312
(610) 647-6970
www.pzarchitects.com